W9-AJS-578

Texas Highways Cookbook

J. Griffis Smith

Texas HIGHWAYS Cookbook

by Joanne Smith
Foreword by Frank Lively

University of Texas Press   Austin

Copyright © 1986 by the University of Texas Press
All rights reserved
Printed in Japan

Second paperback printing, 1994

Requests for permission to reproduce material from this
work should be sent to:
    Permissions
    University of Texas Press
    Box 7819
    Austin, Texas 78713-7819

♾   The paper used in this publication meets the
minimum requirements of American National Standard
for Information Sciences—Permanence of Paper for
Printed Library Materials, ANSI Z39.48-1984.

Library of Congress Cataloging-in-Publication Data

Texas highways cookbook.
        Includes index.
        1. Cookery, American—Southwestern style.
2. Texas—Social life and customs. I. Smith, Joanne,
1931–   . II. Texas Highways (Austin, Tex.)
TX715.T3644   1986   641.59764   86-4949
ISBN 0-292-78088-5 pbk.

To the cowboys who blazed the trails
and gave us the cattle industry.

Acknowledgments

Thanks to the State Department of Highways and Public Transportation for the *Texas Highways* magazine. I applaud its fine staff of editors, writers, and photographers, past and present, especially editor Frank Lively, managing editor Tommie Pinkard, and photographer Jack Lewis. I am also indebted to two other state agencies: The Texas Department of Agriculture and The U.T. Institute of Texan Cultures, for material they have made available for this book as well as for the *Texas Highways* magazine. In addition, I appreciate the cooperation of the magazine's independent food feature sources, such as Fran Gerling, Mary Faulk Koock, and other frequent contributors, as well as a few more cooks around Texas whose recipes are also printed in this book for their relevance, adding extra contrast and color.

J.S.

Contents

© Len Wolff

Foreword

Through the years, *Texas Highways* readers have often written to ask, "Why don't you publish a cookbook of all those fabulous recipes you run?"

We liked the idea, but since we lacked the staff and resources to produce books, we put the idea behind us. We continued to publish food articles in the magazine, and we continued to get those letters.

The letter we published in the February 1985 issue changed everything.

Beverly Walker of Broken Arrow, Oklahoma, wrote: "Have you ever considered compiling a cookbook from the recipes published from time to time? In reading letters in back issues, I came across several referring to David Wade's recipes in an earlier issue. I don't have that one, but it must have been a lulu!"

A good idea, thought Joanne Smith of Dallas. Joanne, a free-lance writer who has written many features for the magazine, immediately sent us a letter outlining the way she thought a *Texas Highways* cookbook should look and sound. We agreed, but explained that we aren't in the book business.

Two months later, the editors at the University of Texas Press in Austin approached us about publishing a book based on the magazine. But what, we asked ourselves, would be the subject? We suggested several possibilities. Then we brought up Joanne's proposal for a cookbook. They liked that idea immediately.

Our readers had suggested that we "compile" a cookbook. One look, however, tells you that Joanne did more than that. She accomplished an outstanding job of creative editing, weaving recipes and features together, rewriting some articles, adding new text, and doing it all in her relaxed, delightful style.

"Beans need to cook forever," she writes, "or until tender, whichever comes first."

Joanne has a clever way of describing foods that makes me think, "I wish I'd said that." You'll enjoy simply thumbing through the pages, trying to decide which recipe to try first.

In reading these pages, I was surprised by the number and variety of recipes published in *Texas Highways* during the past eight years. The dishes vary from Lebanese *kibbe* to that Texas delicacy, chicken-fried steak. Many of the dishes are Texas versions of exotic foods, reflecting immigrants' desires to bring a little bit of home to this new land.

The photographs in this book all appeared in past issues of *Texas Highways*. When I look through them, I recall the problems our photographers had getting some of them—Geoff Appold trying to take photos of Mexican food in the dark, cramped kitchen of a studio apartment in Houston; Jack Lewis photographing a melting whipped cream dessert outdoors under an August sun. And then I look at their scenes of barbecue smoking over a mesquite fire, a heaping bowl of blueberries, a still-life of tree-ripened peaches tumbling from a basket, and I get hungry all over again.

It was a pleasure gathering these recipes and photographs during the last eight years. We hope you'll enjoy them even longer than that.

Frank Lively
Editor, *Texas Highways*

Jack Lewis

Preface

Each month, *Texas Highways* brings into focus all the best there is to do and see in Texas. At the same time, to the delight of hundreds of thousands of readers, the official state travel magazine unreels a spectacular panorama of scenic beauty, intertwined with the agriculture, industry, and population of our many-splendored Lone Star State.

Most of the recipes in this collection have been published in *Texas Highways*, which, of course, issues from the State Department of Highways and Public Transportation. A number of recipes have been borrowed from the Texas Department of Agriculture and the University of Texas Institute of Texan Cultures. These and other previously unpublished, but related, recipes (which have been contributed by good Texas cooks) serve to widen our perspective of the broad spectrum of Texas cuisine. Savor them all against a *Texas Highways* backdrop.

In Texas, when we think of fish, we remember the water splashing against a palm-silhouetted Gulf Coast. The taste of fresh oranges reminds us of a sun-drenched citrus grove in the Rio Grande Valley. We enjoy peach orchards beneath a mantle of pink blossoms and the pastoral green countryside where cattle graze, as well as the tanglewood of mesquite branches and giant pecan trees which flavor some of our favorite fare.

During the peak of immigration years, clusters of new citizens brought their customs and cuisine to the state. From time to time, *Texas Highways* recognizes and salutes these contributions to the overall Texan culture, pulling off the road at New Braunfels for a taste of German wurst, or sniffing the air around the small town of West for the aroma of freshly baked kolaches. Although recipes did not necessarily accompany each of those features, several are included here which have been borrowed from *The Melting Pot*, a collection of ethnic recipes published in 1977 by the U.T. Institute of Texan Cultures. Some recipes from *Romantic Recipes from the Old South*, published by the Imperial Sugar Company in 1950, are scheduled for publication in *Texas Highways* in 1987.

This book reflects the ever-broadening menu of our state. The contemporary Texan may order barbecue and a brew for lunch, and top it off with peach cobbler. The next day, that Texan might enjoy a salad of three kinds of mushrooms marinated in rose-petal vinegar, and *framboises à la crème fraîche*. Phony? No. The big state that welcomed groups of immigrants from all parts of the world and assimilated their customs and cuisine into Texan culture has made room for the *nouvelle cuisine* too. Hence, a few such recipes have been requested from authoritative chefs.

For a time, Texans enjoyed watching the whole world walk a mile in our boots. In fact, we have seen the glitzy fashion era of Texas Chic and poolside barbecue bring a lot of converts to Texas. Once all the designer labels and rhinestones had settled, however, faded jeans and ten-gallon hats came out of the closet again, representing the good life in Texas. Now, barbecue comes back out of the pantry, also, wearing its original chuckwagon pedigree. Somehow, it feels good . . . like coming home.

You don't have to cook to take a culinary trip through the state on *Texas Highways*. Just keep the book handy at your kitchen table and go along for the ride. Cuisine, Texas, lies straight ahead, just beyond the fork.

Joanne Smith

1

First Things First

© Byron Augustin

Appetizers

Texas pecans really are all they're cracked up to be. They may appear before, during, or after any meal, thereby justifying the bragging that Texans do about them. To some, the pecan is a work of culinary art dressed with butter and salt. To others, pecans may be the main substance of a dish. Many Texans believe that if a recipe has any merit at all, pecans can only improve it. Here is a favorite from the pages of *Texas Highways*.

J. Griffis Smith

Texas Pecan Picadillo

1 large onion, finely chopped
1 tablespoon bacon drippings or
    butter
1 pound ground beef
1 clove garlic, minced
1 teaspoon ground cloves
1 teaspoon cinnamon
10-ounce can tomatoes and green
    chiles
1 teaspoon sugar
½ cup raisins
1 teaspoon ground cumin
¾ cup Texas pecans, chopped
salt to taste
corn chips or tostados

Brown onion in the fat. Add beef and brown, stirring to break up. Drain off drippings. Add garlic, cloves, cinnamon, tomatoes, and sugar. Simmer, covered, about 1 hour. Add raisins and cumin and continue to simmer, covered, 20 minutes. Add pecans and simmer 10 more minutes. Salt to taste and serve hot in a chafing dish with corn chips. Recipe yields 1 quart.

Tex-Mex appetizers and short orders may be the most popular snacks in San Antonio, but around that city's St. George Maronite Church, Lebanese Texans celebrate the Middle Eastern gastronomical experience, just as they do in every nook and cranny where the original itinerant immigrants peddled their wares. In November 1981, *Texas Highways* traced their path across Texas.

Amazingly, the turn-of-the-century Lebanese immigrant to Texas was able to make a living selling from door to door in Arabic. With a little bit of Phoenician trader instinct and a lot of tenacity, these immigrants carved a small niche, becoming part of the pattern of the colorful Texan culture.

From "The Lebanese Texans," *Texas Highways*, November 1981:

"A century ago, the occasional Lebanese immigrant must have stood out like a camel in a corral.

The Lebanese had a somewhat unusual appearance, and he spoke Arabic, which he read and wrote from right to left. His taste ran to cracked wheat mixed with uncooked ground lamb, and big, flat loaves of bread. He cooked grapevine leaves folded around a spicy rice and meat filling, and enjoyed sweet black coffee with multi-layered, nutty pastry."

Now, of course, supermarkets carry tahini, tabooley mix, and grapevine leaves packed in salt water, to say nothing of always-available pita bread and bahlawa pastry. But twenty-five years ago, not even Kahlil Gibran's legendary Prophet could have predicted that.

The Lebanese cuisine was developed before flatware; therefore many of the dishes make excellent appetizers served with the flat pita bread, cut or broken into bite-size pieces. These are the recipes Janie Ashmore and her friends have used to raise thousands of dollars in funds for churches in San Antonio and Dallas.

Hummus b'Tahini
(Garbanzo Bean Dip)

15-ounce can garbanzo beans, drained
3 tablespoons tahini (ground sesame
    seeds)
½ cup lemon juice
1 clove crushed garlic
⅛ teaspoon ground cumin (optional)
¾ teaspoon salt, or to taste
¼ cup water
olive oil
chopped parsley

Place drained garbanzos, tahini, lemon juice, crushed garlic, cumin, and salt in blender. Add water and puree, adding more water if necessary to keep mixture from becoming stiff. Mound onto a serving dish and drizzle a small amount of olive oil over the top. Sprinkle a ring of chopped parsley around the edge of the dish. Serve with pieces of Lebanese or pita bread.

Mihshi Waraq Inab
(Stuffed Grapevine Leaves)

¾ cup uncooked rice
6 tablespoons butter
½ teaspoon cinnamon
¼ teaspoon ground cloves
1 tablespoon salt
1 teaspoon black pepper
¾ pound ground lamb or beef
1 jar preserved grapevine leaves
    (1 pound, 9 ounces)
2 cups hot water
1 tablespoon salt
¼ cup lemon juice

Soak rice in hot water to cover about 10 minutes. Drain. Melt 5 tablespoons butter over low heat, reserving 1 tablespoon unmelted. Put drained rice in the melted butter and add seasonings. Remove from heat and mix with the uncooked meat.

To roll: Set aside the oversized or badly torn leaves. Snip any stem ends from the leaves. Spread each leaf flat; place a heaping teaspoon of filling on the stem end of the rough side. Beginning to roll toward the tip, fold side edges over. Continue rolling and squeeze gently.

Place rolled leaves, opening face down, in orderly stacks in a 2½-quart saucepan, lined with some of the large or torn leaves. Add reserved butter and cover with several big leaves. Place a small plate over the leaves to hold rolls in place while cooking. Add 2 cups hot water and 1 tablespoon more salt. Cover and bring water to a boil. Then lower the heat and cook 30 minutes. Add lemon juice and cook 10 more minutes. Drain water; remove plate and large leaves. Remove rolls carefully. Makes about 4 dozen.

Tabbuli (Tabooley)

4 large bunches parsley, finely
    chopped
1 cup fresh mint leaves, or 2
    tablespoons dried mint, chopped
1 bunch green onions, including
    tender green ends, chopped
4 or 5 peeled, chopped tomatoes
1 cup burghol (cracked wheat),
    #2 size
½ cup lemon juice
1 tablespoon salt
pepper to taste
¼ cup olive oil

Clean, wash, and chop vegetables. Wash and soak wheat about 10 minutes. Squeeze water out, and add wheat to vegetable mixture. Add lemon juice, seasonings, and olive oil. Mix well and chill. This may be eaten as a salad, but traditionally it is eaten by gathering a bit onto a fresh, tender grape leaf, a leaf of romaine lettuce, or a piece of bread.

———————

The basic kibbe recipe, made with lean lamb or beef, can be served a number of ways, depending on the occasion and the portion. It can be eaten fried, baked, or raw (like beef tartare). For an hors d'oeuvre, roll into individual football-shaped servings.

Kibbe

2 cups burghol (cracked wheat),
    #2 size grain
1 large onion, minced
½ cup fresh mint leaves, or 2
    tablespoons dried mint, minced
2 tablespoons salt
½ teaspoon pepper
¼ teaspoon cinnamon
1 teaspoon allspice
2 pounds (4 cups) lean lamb or beef,
    ground to a paste

Note: Meat must be absolutely free of fat or gristle and must be mixed with hands dipped in ice water to keep ingredients cold.

Cover burghol with cold water and soak for 10 minutes. Drain and press with palms of hands to remove water. Mince onion and mint together and mix with salt and spices. Knead meat and seasonings together, add burghol, and mix thoroughly.

   The basic recipe can be shaped like hamburger patties and fried in either butter or olive oil, or brushed with butter and baked at 400° F. for 20 minutes, turning only once.

And one more from the Lebanese Texans:

Meat Pie Fingers

Filling
1 pound ground lamb or chuck
1 large onion, sliced thin or chopped
1 tablespoon salt
1 teaspoon pepper
½ cup pine nuts (optional)
1 teaspoon allspice
1 tablespoon lemon juice

Pastry
2½ sticks margarine (1¼ cups)
¾ cup water
4¼ cups flour

In a skillet, combine meat with other filling ingredients, except lemon juice, and cook over medium heat until onion is tender but not brown (about 15 minutes). Add lemon juice and set aside.

   To make pastry, melt margarine, add water and flour, and mix well with hands to consistency of pie dough. Break off into balls about 1 inch in diameter. Roll out each ball into a round and fill with 1 teaspoon filling. Roll up to resemble a finger and pinch ends together. Bake in a 425° F. oven 13–15 minutes, or until lightly browned. Makes about 6–7 dozen. Leftovers may be frozen.

———————

Among the favorite Chinese recipes recorded by the U.T. Institute of Texan Cultures in *The Melting Pot*, this one is always in demand:

Spring Rolls, Sometimes Called Egg Rolls

Wrapping
Fresh egg noodle sheets, also called won ton skins, which can be purchased from Chinese grocers or specialty shops

Filling
3 scallions, sliced
1 cup shredded cabbage
1 cup crisscross shredded celery
2 tablespoons soy sauce
1 teaspoon sugar
1 teaspoon salt
1 teaspoon cornstarch
1 pound pork, cut in shreds
½ pound fresh shrimp, chopped

1 tablespoon cooking oil
additional cooking oil for frying
    (1 inch in frying pan)

Combine first seven ingredients. Stir in pork and shrimp. Stir fry in 1 tablespoon heated oil. When cooked and cooled, place in wrappings, forming rolls. Moisten edge to hold shape. Fry in 1 inch of cooking oil until the outside is crisp and golden. Serve while hot.

———————

In 1982, when *Texas Highways* considered Christmas gifts from the kitchen, combining something homemade with something store-bought, Dusty McGuire, a fine Amarillo cook, gave us this pastry-wrapped brie. A welcome break from ordinary cheese gifts, brie can be wrapped in pastry, decorated with some significant Texana, then refrigerated till time of delivery. It looks wonderful presented on a baking tile or pretty cheeseboard. Include the recipe with the instructions for baking. Or make one for your own enjoyment—don't wait till Christmas.

Brie en Croûte

3-ounce package cream cheese (room
    temperature)
¼ cup butter, softened
¾ cup all-purpose flour, sifted
4½-ounce package brie, whole, with
    skin intact
1 egg yolk mixed with 1 tablespoon
    water
½ teaspoon sesame seeds

In medium bowl, cut cream cheese and butter into flour with a pastry blender or two knives as you would for any pastry, until the granules are the size of small peas. Press pastry into a ball; wrap in foil, and refrigerate for 1 hour or more.

   Divide dough into two circles and roll each about ⅛ inch thick, cutting one about 6 inches across and one about 8 inches across. Set the whole, round brie on the smaller pastry round. Fit the larger round over the top and fold it under the bottom, pressing it together

© Don Heit

Brie en Croûte (on board) and Lone Star Caviar (in glass bowl)

For another non-sweet kitchen gift idea, the Texas Department of Agriculture gave us Lone Star Caviar (also known as pickled black-eyed peas). For a New Year's gift to remember, make this recipe for 7½ cups and take it to the party in a handsome crock or a pretty bowl. But don't save the recipe for the holidays—it's good anytime.

Lone Star Caviar

1 pound dried black-eyed peas
2 cups Italian salad dressing
2 cups diced green pepper
1½ cups diced onion
1 cup finely chopped green onion
½ cup finely chopped jalapeño peppers
3-ounce jar diced pimiento, drained
1 tablespoon finely chopped garlic
salt to taste
hot pepper sauce to taste

Soak black-eyed peas in enough water to cover for 6 hours or overnight. Drain well. Transfer peas to a saucepan; add enough water to cover. Bring to a boil over high heat. Reduce heat and allow to boil until tender, about 45 minutes. Do not overcook. Drain well and transfer to a large bowl. Blend in dressing and let cool. Add remaining ingredients and mix well. Makes 7½ cups.

---

and twisting or crimping all around the edge. Decorate with pastry scraps. Brush entire pastry with egg yolk mixed with water. Sprinkle sesame seeds over the top and refrigerate.

To bake: heat oven to 400° F. and bake about 20 minutes or until golden brown. Let stand for a few minutes before serving.

Ever since people started calling crawdads "crawfish" and giving them an uptown dress, they've been appearing at the best parties. This dip came to *Texas Highways* from Austin home economist Fran Gerling.

Crawfish Dip

4 ounces sour cream
8 ounces cream cheese, softened
1 tablespoon bottled steak sauce
1 teaspoon salt
1 teaspoon black pepper, or more to taste
⅛ teaspoon garlic powder
⅛ teaspoon red pepper, or more to taste

1 pound crawfish tails, cooked and peeled
½ cup celery, chopped
½ cup fresh onion, minced
1 fresh tomato, chopped and drained
4 ounces green chiles, finely chopped
dash of hot sauce, or more to taste

Mix sour cream, cream cheese, and steak sauce together in a mixer or food processor. Blend in salt, black pepper, garlic powder, and red pepper. With a spatula, fold in remaining ingredients; then taste and adjust seasonings. If there is time, refrigerate for an hour. Serve with corn chips.

Note: Buy 6–7 pounds live crawfish to produce 1 pound of tails for the above recipe. To prepare crawfish: wash first; discard dead ones. Fill your biggest pot with water; bring to a rapid boil, add crawfish, and cook 5 minutes. Cool. Separate tail from head by twisting and pulling; discard head. Crack the shell by squeezing the tail with your thumb and forefinger. Remove the first three segments and loosen the meat. Holding the last segment and tail fin with one hand, pull the meat with the other.

This is good anytime:

Chili-Cheese Log

3-ounce package cream cheese
2 cups shredded American cheese
1 tablespoon lemon juice
¼ teaspoon garlic powder
¼ cup pecans, finely chopped
1 teaspoon chili powder
1 teaspoon paprika

Let cheeses stand at room temperature to soften. Combine cheeses, lemon juice, and garlic powder. Beat with mixer or food processor until well blended. Stir in pecans. Shape into a roll about 1½ inches in diameter. Sprinkle roll with mixture of chili powder and paprika. Refrigerate. Let stand at room temperature 10 minutes before serving with crackers.

Soups

In January 1986, *Texas High-ways* snooped into soup pots around the state, pointing out that Texans like all kinds of soup, from sweet and chilling to cheap but filling . . . and published five recipes to prove it. Ask any ranch cook, though— we probably have as many kinds of soup as we have of "bob war." The first soup at right came from the British Sideboard, Corpus Christi.

J. Griffis Smith

Tortilla Soup, as the Tigua Indians make it

Chilled Peach Soup

12 peaches, peeled and sliced
1 cup sugar
½ cup lemon juice
½ cup orange juice
½ cup sherry
4 cups sour cream

Mix peaches and sugar in blender until smooth. Add juices, sherry, and sour cream; blend well. Chill several hours or overnight before serving. Eight servings.

Here's soup you can get your teeth into, from frequent *Texas Highways* contributor Fran Gerling.

Brisket Soup

1 pound lean brisket, trimmed well
2 teaspoons oil
1 quart water
1 teaspoon salt, or more
¼ teaspoon black pepper
3 carrots, pared and cut in thick rounds
1 zucchini squash
1 yellow squash
½ cup pearl onions
1 medium tomato, cut in wedges

Cut brisket into bite-size pieces. In a large Dutch oven, heat oil and brown meat on all sides. Add water, salt, pepper, and carrots; simmer, covered, for 1 hour. Meanwhile, slit squashes lengthwise and then cut in chunks. Add onions, squashes, and tomato wedges to soup. Cover and simmer for 30 minutes more. Taste and adjust seasonings before serving. Makes five 1-cup servings.

This soup doubles or triples very well and keeps in the refrigerator for 3 or 4 days. It also freezes well.

Note: It may be necessary to ask the butcher to custom cut the brisket in order to get a lean piece. Normally, the brisket that we smoke or barbecue has layers of fat in it. If you use a fatty brisket, plan to skim the fat off when the soup cools. *Do not use smoked brisket.*

The name may be misleading, but East Texas Depression Turkey Soup was intended to treat financial rather than emotional problems. *Texas Highways* traces the soup's origin to the Great Depression years following the Market Crash of 1929. At the time, the charm of the recipe lay in the fact that it calls for little more than a leftover turkey carcass, and the soup can be extended to have a different taste and appearance the following day. It's still not a bad idea . . . and you can always add anything you like.

East Texas Depression Turkey Soup

3 quarts turkey (or chicken) broth
3–4 cups turkey chunks
2 large onions, chopped
½ cup pearl onions (optional)
6 stalks celery, chopped
2 tablespoons parsley
salt and pepper to taste
    Second Day
6-ounce can tomato paste
1–2 cups cooked rice, depending on amount of soup left

Make 3 quarts of broth using a leftover turkey (or chicken) carcass or bouillon cubes. Remove bones and add 3–4 cups turkey chunks; allow to simmer for 1 hour. Add onions, celery, and parsley, and simmer 30 minutes or until the vegetables are tender. Add salt and pepper to taste and serve.

The next day, add to the remaining soup the tomato paste and cooked rice. Simmer 20 minutes.

Another from the magazine:

Potato and Parsley Soup

1 large Bermuda onion, sliced
3 tablespoons butter
5 medium to large (5-inch) potatoes, peeled and sliced
4–5 cups chicken stock
1–2 cups half-and-half cream
½ cup snipped parsley (or more)
salt and pepper
parsley and carrot slivers, for garnish

Slice onion and sauté in skillet with butter until tender but not brown. Add thinly sliced potatoes, and cook covered in chicken stock (instant is fine) until done, 15 minutes or so. Cool. Blend a small portion at a time with cream until it is the consistency you prefer. Add snipped parsley and process in blender until thoroughly refined. Season with salt and pepper to taste and chill. Serve ice cold or hot, with a good white wine. Garnish with parsley and thin carrot slivers. Serves 6–8.

When *Texas Highways'* Tommie Pinkard visited Los Patios in San Antonio, she found a vast nursery full of blooming marvels, a shopping gallery, and three restaurants. One of the restaurants served this soup.

Los Patios Cheese Soup

3 chopped green onions
3 stalks chopped celery, some leaves
2 grated carrots
¼ cup butter or margarine
2 10¾-ounce cans chicken broth
3 10¾-ounce cans condensed potato soup
8 ounces grated yellow cheese
parsley flakes
salt to taste
coarse grind pepper to taste
⅛ teaspoon Tabasco sauce, or to taste
8 ounces sour cream
3 tablespoons sherry

Sauté onions, celery, and carrots in the melted butter. Add chicken broth and simmer 30 minutes. Add potato soup, cheese, parsley, salt, pepper, and Tabasco. Stir in sour cream and simmer 15 minutes. Add sherry, stir, and serve. Makes 10 cups.

Cheese-Broccoli Soup

For a delicious cheese-broccoli soup, puree ingredients in an electric blender before adding sour cream. With sour cream, add one 10-ounce package frozen broccoli tips, cooked until just tender. Simmer 15 minutes, add sherry, stir, and serve.

Researching the old-time Texas Christmas with archaeologist Daphne Derven for *Texas Highways* in 1984 turned up a couple of soup selections from early cookbooks. Daphne made corn soup in a big kettle on the hearth of the Old City Park log cabin, in Dallas, on one occasion, and venison soup on another. Both recipes are worth saving, although you might want to update them with modern-day touches of your own.

Corn Soup

Grate 2 ears of corn to each pint of water. Six quarts would make a good tureen of soup. Add 1 pound of pork, black and red pepper, salt and herb powder, and 2 chopped onions and 2 carrots for each pound of pork. Stew for several hours.

Venison Soup

Take 4 pounds of freshly killed venison cut off from the bones, and 1 pound of ham in small slices. Add an onion minced, and black pepper to your taste. Put only as much water as will cover it, and stew it gently for an hour, keeping the pot closely covered. Then skim it well, and pour in a quart of boiling water. Add a head of celery cut into small pieces, and half a dozen blades of mace. Boil it gently 2½ hours. Then put in ¼ pound of butter, divided into small pieces and rolled in flour, and ½ pint of port or Madeira wine. Let it boil a quarter of an hour longer, and send it to table with the meat in it.

You may have driven within a mile of Panna Maria and never known it was there. The oldest permanent Polish settlement in America, named for a church in Krakow, Poland, keeps a low profile, with only one church and one store/post office, but *Texas Highways* found it. Since its beginning, the tiny village has survived on little more than faith and endurance. The store originally was a barn, built in 1855.

The stone church was erected in 1878, although its site had been selected on Christmas Eve 1854, when the first seven hundred Polish immigrants arrived.

The U.T. Institute of Texan Cultures estimates the current population of Polish-Texans at a quarter of a million, who have kept intact traditions related to their religion, such as Christmas celebrations and weddings, and their cuisine. Here's a Polish soup recipe, from the Institute's book *The Melting Pot*.

Easy Barszcz (Beet Soup)

12 medium beets
1 medium onion, sliced
1 quart water
juice of 1 lemon
1 tablespoon sugar
salt and pepper to taste
2 cups bouillon
½ cup sour cream

Wash and peel beets. Cook beets and onion in water until beets are tender. Add lemon juice, sugar, salt, and pepper. Let stand overnight. Strain. Add bouillon and sour cream. Reheat and serve with uszka (see p. 75). Six 1-cup servings.

The aroma of soup simmering in a big pot on the range warms the heart on a cold day. If you save your hambones for the right weather report, you'll want to make my split pea soup on the next foggy day.

Thicker-than-Fog Pea Soup

½ hambone, along with any leftover bits of ham
1 quart boiling water
1 bay leaf
⅛ teaspoon thyme
¼ teaspoon celery seed
1 cup dried green split peas (washed, not soaked)
½ cup grated carrots
1 peeled tomato, or ½ cup canned tomatoes
1 cup milk or cream

Remove as much meat as possible from the bone and save meat to be added later. Crack the bone and place it in water in a soup kettle. Add seasonings, peas, carrots, and tomato. Cover and simmer 1–1½ hours. Remove the bone and strain soup, pressing peas through a sieve. Stir in milk or cream and extra bits of ham. Reheat gently. Do not allow to boil after adding milk or cream.

Credit the success of the following Cream of Pecan Soup to Mrs. Trammell Crow, who plays an important part in the daily activities of Loews Anatole Hotel and the Dallas Market Center, which was developed by her husband. She proposed the very successful soup recipe for the hotel's elegant L'Entrecote restaurant.

Make the soup a day ahead, if possible. Overnight storage strengthens the pecan flavor.

Cream of Pecan Soup

1 cup finely chopped celery
1 cup finely chopped onions
½ cup + 1 tablespoon butter
½ pound crushed pecans
2 teaspoons salt
½ teaspoon freshly ground white pepper
1 small garlic clove, minced
2 ounces dark rum
2 ounces whiskey
3 ounces white wine
8 cups chicken stock
1½ tablespoons arrowroot or cornstarch
4 tablespoons whipped cream

In a high-sided soup pot, sauté celery and onions in butter until golden, add pecans, and cook 4–5 minutes longer. Add salt, freshly ground white pepper, and garlic.

Add rum, whiskey, white wine, and chicken stock. Simmer over low heat for about 2 hours. Correct seasonings.

Dissolve arrowroot in 3 tablespoons water and mix into the soup. Cook for 10 more minutes. Stir occasionally to keep from sticking. Blend the soup well while still hot. Check the seasoning, and serve in hot soup bowls with a dollop of whipped cream on top. Serves 4.

In June 1981, when *Texas Highways* celebrated Black Heritage Day, which old-timers still call Juneteenth, some Texas frontier history came to light. For instance, in 1519, Cortez had three hundred black soldiers to help him conquer the Aztecs. By 1791, 24 percent of the Texas population was black, but only about a hundred were listed in the census as slaves. Ironically, slave owners didn't move in until Texas became a *free* republic.

After the Civil War, three to five thousand blacks became trail-riding Texas cowboys. Mathew "Bones" Hooks started out breaking horses. Later, he became popular as a civic leader and organizer of the Amarillo Boys Club. Bill Pickett, one of the greatest cowboy showmen, invented the rodeo technique called "bulldogging" and toured Europe with his act. These and other black cowhands have their names recorded in the history of herding cattle.

After the Civil War, some of the freedmen became sought-after trail-riders as cooks. Often, they were the only ones who had any skill with cooking a good pot of beans, or who knew how to prepare small animals available on the range. The job was important to the trail ride. Tommie Pinkard wrote:

"Cowboys considered the cook's reputation when deciding which cattle drive to sign on for. Cooks were well paid since they also functioned as barbers, dentists, and physicians as well as arbiters of disputes."

The frontier predecessor of "soul food" was as well received at the time as it is now. The following recipe is from *The Melting Pot*, published by the U.T. Institute of Texan Cultures.

John Suhrstedt

Madeline Hopkins, of San Antonio, celebrates Juneteenth in plantation-era costume, with her grandchildren.

Hambone Soup

1 hambone with meat
2 large onions, diced
3 stalks celery
3 carrots
1 pound tomatoes
3 potatoes, cubed
2 whole cloves
1 cup snap beans, broken
1 cup butter beans
¼ cup diced turnips
½ cup green peas
1 tablespoon sugar
salt and pepper
1 cup fresh corn kernels

Cover the hambone with water in a large kettle. Boil until meat is almost tender. Add remaining ingredients, except the corn. Cover and cook slowly for 3–4 hours. Add corn during the last 15 minutes of cooking. Makes about 8 servings.

The last soup recipe is from Dusty McGuire of Amarillo.

Tortilla Soup

1 medium onion, chopped
2 garlic cloves, minced
2 tablespoons vegetable oil
14½-ounce can chicken broth (uncondensed)
14½-ounce can beef broth (uncondensed)
10½-ounce can condensed tomato soup
16-ounce jar mild picante sauce
14½-ounce can tomatoes, pureed
2 teaspoons Worcestershire sauce
1 teaspoon ground cumin
1 teaspoon chili powder
6 corn tortillas, cut into ½-inch wedges
Cheddar cheese, grated

Cook onion and garlic in oil till onion is tender. Add remaining ingredients except tortillas and cheese. Bring to boil, reduce heat, and simmer uncovered 30 minutes. Add tortilla wedges and simmer about 5 minutes. Ladle into bowls and top with cheese.

2

Main Dishes

TDA

Fish and Seafood

Old-time fishers of Texas rivers can tell you tales of 50- or 60-pound catfish. They can tell you about carving the skinned flanks into strips, rolling them in seasoned white cornmeal, then deep-frying them to a light golden brown.

That's still the best way to prepare catfish, determines Dallas restaurant critic Betty Cook, although the sophisticated palate may prefer the mousse invented by Stephan Pyles at the Routh Street Cafe in Dallas and served with crayfish sauce.

"My regional forebears would have loved it," says Betty, "if any of them would have been caught paying $37.50 for dinner. Which they would not. They wouldn't have eaten crayfish sauce, either; they called them crawdads and used them for bait . . . catfish was poor folks' fish. Anyone could afford it; it was caught, not bought."

Now that smaller catfish is farmed, should it be fried whole (new style) or fileted (old style)? The best of both worlds, according to Betty Cook, is to butterfly the fish, semi-separating boneless sides from the backbone so the cornmeal can coat every surface of the succulent meat.

"Result: Every bite is a sybaritic symphony of moist, evenly cooked flesh wrapped in crunch."

The Matagorda Island lighthouse dates from 1852.

Once in an affluent while, even the serious catfisher enjoys the Mansion on Turtle Creek, just for the halibut. With the recipe below, you can dress up at home and remember dining at the Dallas jewel in the Rosewood chain.

Mansion Halibut with Cashews and Mango-Basil Sauce

½ pound roasted cashews, ground fine
1 cup dry bread crumbs
4 6-ounce portions of skinless, boneless halibut or other firm white fish
salt to taste
3–4 tablespoons peanut oil

Make the sauce (below) first and keep warm in a double boiler. Preheat oven to 375° F. Combine ground cashews and bread crumbs in a medium-size bowl. Season portions of halibut and press into crumb mixture until completely coated. Sauté in oil over medium heat until lightly brown. Turn fish over with a spatula and switch the pan to the oven. Bake about 8 minutes or until the fish is firm. Do not overcook. Remove from oven and place fish in center of warm plates, surrounding the fish with mango-basil sauce. Serve at once. Serves 4.

Mango-Basil Sauce

3 large, ripe mangoes, peeled and seeds removed
3 cups chicken stock
1 cup heavy cream
1 large bunch fresh basil, washed clean and tied with string
salt and lime juice to taste

Using a large saucepan, bring mango, stock, and cream to a boil, then simmer 20 minutes to reduce volume by half. Pour mixture into a blender and mix until smooth. Add basil bouquet and keep warm over hot water until ready to serve. Then remove basil and season with salt and lime juice.

Another from Fran Gerling:

Seafood-Stuffed Redfish

1 tablespoon butter
¼ cup minced green onion (white part)
¼ cup celery, minced
1 tablespoon pimiento, minced
½ pound fresh shrimp, boiled, shelled, and chopped
1 cup fresh bread crumbs
2 eggs, beaten
½ teaspoon salt
¼ teaspoon white pepper
dash cayenne pepper
4-pound redfish, head removed, and preferably boned by butcher
salt and pepper to taste
melted butter (optional)
garnish: leaf lettuce with fresh pimientos or cherry tomatoes

Melt butter in skillet and sauté onion and celery. Transfer to mixing bowl, and add pimiento, shrimp, bread crumbs, eggs, salt, white pepper, and cayenne; blend well. Prepare redfish by sprinkling salt and pepper inside cavity and place the fish in a baking pan. Add stuffing. Brush with a little melted butter if desired. Bake at 350° F. for about 30 minutes or until fish flakes easily with a fork. Transfer to a platter lined with leaf lettuce. Garnish fish with fresh pimientos or cherry tomatoes. If the fish has bones, remove them by carefully pulling out the fins. Cut across fish starting from backbone area and beware of small rib bones. Serves 5.

Note: Sometimes, with plenty of notice, the butcher will remove the backbone and most bones inside the fish for you. If that service is not available to you, this recipe also works well with filets of flounder, redfish, and sole.

Bonnie Spelling at the Sherry Inn, south of Jefferson, gave *Texas Highways* this recipe for shrimp curry, as served in the Gazebo Room:

Easy Shrimp Curry

2 pounds fresh raw shrimp

Peel and devein shrimp; sauté lightly in butter with a dash of lemon juice until shrimp is pink (about 4 minutes). Pour on curry sauce.

Curry Sauce

10¾-ounce can cream of shrimp soup
10¾-ounce can cream of mushroom soup
1 cup sour cream
1 teaspoon curry powder (or more, to taste)
2 tablespoons chopped parsley

Mix ingredients well, add to sautéed shrimp, and heat, but do not boil. Serve on a bed of fluffy rice. Serves 8.

In Southeast Texas, where Cajun cooking is the only way, legends, recipes, and jokes all have two primary ingredients: a Cajun accent and crawfish. In March 1981, Randy Mallory and Sallie Evans showed us how the good times roll in the 20 percent Cajun Golden Triangle.

Renée Sonnier's Crawfish Etouffée

½ cup margarine
salt and pepper
1 pound crawfish tails (or shrimp), boiled and peeled
1 medium onion, chopped
1 tablespoon green onion, chopped
2 cloves garlic, chopped
½ bell pepper, chopped
1 tablespoon paprika
1 tablespoon parsley
2 cups water
salt and pepper

Melt margarine in deep frying pan. Salt and pepper the crawfish tails, and cook in margarine 2–3 minutes. Remove crawfish and set aside. Add to frying pan the onions (both kinds), garlic, bell pepper, paprika, and parsley. Sauté well for at least 10 minutes. Return crawfish to pan. Add water, salt, and pepper. Cook slowly for about 40 minutes, stirring occasionally. Serve over rice. Serves 4–6.

Here's another version of the same dish:

Fran Gerling's Crawfish Etouffée

4 tablespoons oil
3 tablespoons flour
1 medium onion
2 tablespoons green pepper, minced
½ cup celery, minced
1½ cups water
1 large tomato, finely chopped or
    pureed
1½ pounds crawfish tails and fat
1 teaspoon salt
1 teaspoon black pepper
⅛ teaspoon cayenne pepper
minced green onion for garnish

Combine oil and flour in a large skillet. Cook mixture over medium heat, stirring constantly, until roux is the color of light caramel, about 10 minutes. Remove skillet from heat. Add onion, green pepper, and celery and stir them in the roux until they are wilted. Place skillet over low heat and add water gradually to make a smooth gravy. Add tomato and crawfish and continue cooking gently for about 10 minutes. Adjust seasonings to taste. Serve over hot fluffy rice. Pass the green onions for garnish. Serves 4 or 5.

———————————————

From Fran DeCoux Gerling, who remembers the Old Country (Louisiana), to *Texas Highways*:

Boiled Crawfish for a Crowd

45–50 pounds live crawfish
4 gallons water in large stock pot
1 box salt (1 pound, 10 ounces)
cayenne pepper to taste
3 packages crab boil seasoning
4 whole onions
4 lemons, halved
½ cup vinegar

Wash crawfish and discard any dead ones. Bring water to a boil and add all other ingredients except crawfish. Let seasoning simmer a few minutes, and then add first batch of crawfish (2–3 quarts). Cover and cook 15 minutes. Turn off heat and let crawfish rest in the broth about 10 minutes. Remove crawfish with a strainer, bring stock back to boil, and add next batch of crawfish. Use the same water for all the crawfish.

Serve in the shell. Let guests peel their own and dip into cocktail sauce or melted butter mixed with lemon juice and garlic powder.

Cocktail Sauce

½ cup chili sauce
½ cup catsup
½ cup horseradish
1½ teaspoons Worcestershire sauce
¼ teaspoon salt
½ cup celery, minced fine
2 teaspoons lemon juice
hot sauce or cayenne pepper to taste

Mix ingredients thoroughly. Will be sufficient for 3–4 pounds of crawfish tails.

Crawfish Delight

1 green pepper, slivered
1 large onion, chopped
¾ cup oil
1½–2 pounds boiled crawfish tails
2 cups raw rice
10-ounce can Rotel tomatoes (with
    chile peppers)
10¾-ounce can cream of celery soup
salt and pepper to taste
4 cups water

Mix all ingredients and pour into a large greased casserole. Bake at 350° F. for 30 minutes. Stir and return to the oven for an additional 15 minutes. Serves 12.

———————————————

If you live on the Gulf Coast and like blue crabs, you probably have spent many a lazy afternoon at the water's edge, like writer Jackie Weger, who reported in the October 1981 issue of *Texas Highways*:

"Unlike other water sports and fishing, crabbing calls for little energy, even less equipment and no fishing license. All you need to land dinner is a chicken neck tied firmly to a string, a thimbleful of patience to wait for a crab to nibble on the bait, and a scoop net to haul in the catch."

Boiled Crab #1

To cook crabs, rinse them live with fresh water (use tongs). Bring a gallon or two of clean water to a full rolling boil in a large pot or old washtub. Add ¼ cup rock salt or ½ cup regular table salt. Add a package of crab boil seasoning. As soon as the boiling water releases the fragrance of the herbs and seasonings, use tongs to put the crabs into the boiling water. Hold each one under for a second or two. Immediately, you will see its olive green shell begin to turn fiery red. Continue adding crabs until the pot is full. Cook at a full boil for about 25 minutes. Lift the crabs out. Eat hot or iced down. If you had a good run of luck crabbing and need to cook a second batch, you can use the seasoned water again.

Boiled Crab #2

Some people prefer another method for preparing crab. Remove the claws with pliers as soon as each crab is caught, and eviscerate the crab by scraping out with a paring knife the small triangular area at the back of the bottom shell. Put the crab and the claws in a bucket of fresh water diluted with table salt (½ cup salt to 5 gallons of water). Keep crabs in the salt water until you cook them in boiling water.

To eat crabs, lift off the back of the crab with a knife. Scrape away loose tissue at the sides and down the middle. Break it in half. Draw out the succulent white meat with a small fork or nut pick. Crack open the crab claw with a nutcracker, or hit it sharply with a knife handle. If you do it just right, the entire muscle comes out whole. Delicious!

Crab Gumbo

1½ cups chopped onions
3 tablespoons vegetable oil
¼ cup flour
3 cups oysters
5 cups fish stock
28-ounce can tomatoes
10-ounce package frozen okra, sliced
1 teaspoon salt
2 teaspoons lemon pepper
¼ teaspoon cayenne pepper
⅓ teaspoon black pepper

bouquet garni (of herbs like thyme,
  bay leaf)
½ pound boneless whitefish, cubed
½ pound shrimp, peeled and deveined
½ pound crab fingers or crab meat
1 tablespoon gumbo filé powder
6 cups cooked rice

Sauté onions in oil until light brown.
Add flour and cook, stirring constantly
until flour browns. Drain and save liquid
from oysters; stir oyster liquid, fish
stock, tomatoes, okra, and seasonings
into the onion-flour mixture. Cook covered 30 minutes; add fish, shrimp, crab,
and oysters. Continue cooking 10 minutes until shrimp are pink and oysters
curl; remove bouquet garni. Just before
serving add gumbo filé. Never let gumbo
boil after filé is added. Serve in shallow
bowls with rice. Serves 12.

In October 1984, *Texas Highways*
brought oyster lovers to the very
edge with advice for scouting, catch-
ing, and sorting oysters, as researched by feature writers Larry
Hodge and Sally Victor. From Matagorda and Aransas, where oystering is a way of life, they wrote a
completely unbiased account:

"... Louisiana. Shucks. People
in the know will tell you that Louisiana oysters aren't fit to pump water
in the same ocean with Texas oysters. Texas oysters are bigger . . .
better . . . etc."

To this day, no one has identified
the brave, curious, or starving ad-
venturer who first ate an oyster,
but according to Annette Hegen,
seafood consumer education spe-
cialist, American Indians left great
piles of the shells along the shores.

They probably prepared them
over a driftwood campfire burned
down to the coals. If you try their
method, place unopened oysters di-
rectly on the coals. After a minute,
steam will bubble from the edge of
the shells, opening them slightly.

If you buy oysters in the shells,
be sure they are tightly closed and
have been taken from safe waters.
If you go oystering, ask the nearest
Texas Parks and Wildlife for a license and advice.

© Mike Flahive

Oysters on the Half-Shell with Caper Sauce

Oysters—An Open and Shut Case

Here's the Hodge-Victor method for
stripping the oyster down to the half-
shell. Start with a pair of heavy cot-
ton gloves and a knife with a sharp but
sturdy blade, and grasp the oyster
firmly by its thicker end, flatter side up.

"Strike the oyster a couple of sharp
blows with the point of the knife at the
thin end of the shell (the end away from
your hand). This will flake off some shell
and allow you to work the knife point
between the halves of the shell.

"Twist the knife to force the shell
open. Then slide the blade inside, along
the upper shell, and slice the muscle at-
taching the oyster. He will surrender at
this point, and you can remove the top
shell. Then cut the muscle attached to
the bottom shell."

Once the oysters have surrendered,
here's what you do:

One-Ton Oysters

wonton wraps
oysters
cream cheese
garlic salt

Quarter oysters. On each wonton wrap
place a piece of oyster and a small hunk
of cream cheese. Sprinkle with garlic
salt. Gather dough and press togetl.er
to seal edges. Drop into hot fat (325° F.)
and fry until golden brown.

Oysters Rosa are served at Charlotte Plummer's Seafare Restaurant in Fulton. The recipe was developed for the 1984 Oyster Fest.

Oysters Rosa

For each serving, place 6 oysters on the half-shell on a baking sheet. Add to each a dash of Worcestershire sauce and ½ teaspoon garlic butter. Broil until firm, about 3 minutes. Arrange on a plate; top each with 1 tablespoon of hot cheese sauce (below) and a sprinkle of toasted bread crumbs.

Cheese Sauce

In the top of a double boiler, melt chunks of processed cheese. Stir, and add ¼ cup milk per pound of cheese.

Oysters on the Half-Shell with Caper Sauce

36 oysters, shucked, with shells
4 slices cooked bacon, drained and crumbled
¼ cup butter (or margarine)
1 tablespoon lemon juice
3 tablespoons pimiento, chopped
4 tablespoons black olives, finely chopped
⅓ cup bread crumbs
for garnish: minced olives, pimientos, and bacon bits

Place oysters on the shells. Combine bacon, butter, lemon juice, pimiento, and olives. Place 1 teaspoon of the mix on each oyster and top with bread crumbs. Garnish with minced olives, pimientos, and bacon bits. Bake on rock salt at 450° F. for 5–7 minutes. Serve with caper sauce.

Caper Sauce

1 cup parsley, minced
¼ cup green onions, chopped
2 tablespoons capers
1 clove garlic
¼ cup mayonnaise
1 tablespoon lemon juice
½ tablespoon prepared mustard

Combine parsley, onions, capers, and garlic in blender. Then mix in the mayonnaise, lemon juice, and mustard. Refrigerate sauce and serve cold with oysters on the half shell.

When *Texas Highways* peeked through kitchen windows in Bosque County, which was established by Norwegian immigrants, we saw smorgasbord and lutefisk in a new light. Leave those complex preparations to the Norwegians, and try this fish loaf we borrowed from the U.T. Institute of Texan Cultures to represent the Norwegian taste.

Fish Pudding

2 pounds haddock
2 tablespoons potato flour
1 teaspoon salt
¼ teaspoon mace
½ cup cream
¼ cup melted butter

Grind fish three times, then add potato flour, salt, and mace. Beat the fish into a heavy paste as cream is added. Then add butter. Place in a greased casserole and bake in a container of water in the oven as you would bake custard. Cover with brown paper so the top does not burn. Bake at 350° F. for 40 minutes. Remove from the oven and slice the loaf. Garnish with parsley, paprika, and lemon wedges. Makes 6–8 servings.

Wherever you find okra, you find seafood or chicken gumbo. Fran DeCoux Gerling invents Texas recipes with a Louisiana flavor. Below, she shares her favorite for making seafood gumbo. If you don't have fresh, tender okra, or at least fresh frozen, wait until some other time to make gumbo. Or leave the okra out, if you have enough seafood.

Acadian Seafood Gumbo

½ cup plus 2 tablespoons cooking oil
1 cup flour
1 cup onions, chopped
2 cloves garlic, minced
¼ cup green bell pepper, minced
¼ cup red bell pepper, minced
¼ cup celery, minced
1 cup fresh okra, sliced
½ cup chopped tomatoes

3 quarts shrimp stock (recipe follows), or fish or chicken stock
¼ teaspoon oregano
1 teaspoon salt
1 bay leaf
½ teaspoon black pepper
¼ teaspoon white pepper
½ teaspoon cayenne pepper
1 pound fresh shrimp, peeled
1 pint crab claws, fresh or frozen
12 fresh oysters, shucked
½ cup chopped green onion
1 tablespoon gumbo filé powder

Heat ½ cup oil in a heavy skillet until very hot. Add flour and stir continually to blend over low heat until roux is a dark caramel color, about 30–45 minutes. (Immediately remove any bits of blackened flour because they will cause the roux to be bitter.) Remove skillet from heat and add onions, garlic, green and red bell pepper, and celery. Stir vegetables until wilted. Sauté the okra and tomatoes in 2 tablespoons oil in a separate skillet.

Pour roux mixture, okra and tomatoes, and shrimp stock into large soup pot. Add oregano, salt, bay leaf, black and white pepper, and cayenne; stir and bring mixture to boil. Simmer for 1 hour to blend in the peppers and develop the flavors. Add water as necessary to maintain 3 quarts liquid. Add shrimp and crab claws; continue cooking for 15 minutes. Pour in oysters and green onion. Simmer for 10 minutes. Add filé powder to gumbo just before serving. Ladle gumbo over bowls of rice. Makes eight or nine 1-cup servings.

Note: Never boil gumbo after adding filé powder or it will become stringy.

Shrimp Stock

shrimp heads and shells from 1 pound fresh shrimp
1 medium onion
2 stalks celery
3 quarts water
carcasses and heads of two 4-pound fish

Pour all ingredients into large Dutch oven or soup pot and bring to boil. Simmer 4–6 hours. Strain stock, cool, and set aside or refrigerate for later use.

Poultry

When writer Gary Woolever investigated what was stewing in Hopkins County for the September 1985 issue of *Texas Highways*, he found some concoctions bubbling in big, black caldrons over open fires. Hopkins County Stew, he discovered, dates back to the county's beginning in 1846. Preparation of the dish begins with about 10 or 12 chickens and ends with gallons of the stew. Hopkins County Stew stood as a top contender against chili as the official state dish.

Every pioneer had the first essential qualification to make the dish, the big iron kettle that could be used for washing clothes or brewing a stew. Early East Texas farmers welcomed their neighbors with it; the recipe makes a LOT.

Jack Lewis

Each year contestants vie for the award at the Hopkins County Cookoff. Here are winners from 1983 and 1984. When you decide to make Hopkins County Stew, if you don't want to make 10 or 20 gallons over a fire in the back yard, then reduce the ingredients proportionately to suit your kitchen range.

Hopkins County Stew, 1984 Winner

(by Polly Walters and Glenda Mitchell)

12 4-pound fryers
2 46-ounce cans tomato juice
2 ounces chili powder
1 gallon chicken stock (from cooking chickens)
½ gallon water
1 gallon canned whole tomatoes
10 pounds onions, chopped
1 tablespoon chicken base (chicken bouillon granules)
30 pounds potatoes, cut in chunks
1 gallon canned whole kernel corn
2 tablespoons salt (or to taste)

Cook chickens in large stockpots in water to cover; reserve stock. Bone and marinate the meat in tomato juice and chili powder. Bring stock and water to boil; add tomatoes, onions, and chicken base. Bring to boil. Add chicken and potatoes; simmer 20 minutes or until potatoes are tender. Add corn and salt to taste, and heat through.

Hopkins County Stew, 1982–1983 Winner

(by Charlie and Mary Charles)

10 large chickens
20 pounds potatoes
15 pounds onions
1 46-ounce can V-8 juice
3 46-ounce cans tomato juice
1 large chile pepper, or to taste
2 pounds butter
4-ounce can green chile peppers
½–1 cup sugar, to taste
2 gallons cream-style corn
salt to taste

Bring water to boil in the caldron. Cook and bone chicken meat. Add all other ingredients except corn and salt. Use enough water to cover, and simmer until vegetables are tender. Thirty minutes before serving, add corn. Salt to taste.

———————————

The chicken pot pie recipe from the Imperial Sugar oldies collection (*Romantic Recipes from the Old South*) is worth the time it takes. The tasty pot pie seems to have been designed for the noon meal of starving field hands.

Chicken Pot Pie

3-pound chicken
2 quarts chicken broth and water
1 onion, chopped
1 carrot, sliced and chopped
salt and pepper
2 medium potatoes
2 or 3 carrots
1 or 2 medium onions
¼–½ cup flour

Cover the chicken with broth and water. Add chopped onion and carrot, salt and pepper to taste, and heat to boiling. Reduce and simmer for an hour or until tender (do not allow to boil).

Meanwhile, pare and cube the remaining vegetables and cook in a small amount of water until they can be pierced easily with a fork.

If time allows, cool chicken in broth; if not, remove immediately to a large bowl. Remove and discard the skin and bones; cut the chicken in large dice. Chill the broth, if possible, so you can remove the fat to use in making the sauce and the pastry for the pot pie.

To make the sauce: Combine the vegetable cooking liquid and chicken broth. Melt ¼ cup chicken fat in a skillet; add ¼–½ cup flour, stirring, and cook until bubbly. Add 3–4 cups of chicken broth, stirring to prevent lumping, until a thick, creamy sauce forms.

Layer chicken and vegetables in a large flat casserole or baking dish. Pour sauce over chicken. Top with a tender, flaky pastry (below) and bake at 400° F. about 12–15 minutes, or until crust is well browned.

Pastry

2 cups all-purpose flour
4 teaspoons baking powder
½ teaspoon salt
½ cup chicken fat (or shortening)
⅔ cup milk

Combine dry ingredients and cut in chicken fat. Add milk and stir with fork to make dough. Roll out and place over chicken and vegetables. Serves 6–8 polite Sunday dinner folks.

———————————

From the National Pecan Marketing Council, Bryan:

Chicken Crepes Pecan

24 crepes, prepared from standard recipe or pancake mix
Cream Sauce
½ cup butter
½ cup flour
4 cups milk, scalded
1½ teaspoons salt
¼ teaspoon white pepper

Melt butter; gradually add flour. Cook over low heat, stirring constantly, until well blended. Gradually add milk and continue stirring with a wire whip until thick and smooth. Add salt and pepper; simmer 5 minutes.

Chicken Pecan Filling

3 cups cooked chicken, chopped
1½ tablespoons fresh parsley, chopped
½ cup onion, chopped
1 cup light cream, divided
2 egg yolks
4 cups cream sauce (recipe above)
1 teaspoon salt
1½ cups chopped pecans

Simmer chicken, parsley, and onion in ¾ cup cream for 5 minutes. Combine beaten egg yolks with half the cream sauce. Add to chicken mixture. Add salt and 1 cup chopped pecans. Cook over low heat until mixture is thickened. Spread generous tablespoon of filling down center of each crepe; roll up, leaving ends open. Place crepes seam side down in a buttered baking dish. Stir ¼ cup cream into remaining sauce to thin. Pour over crepes. Sprinkle with remaining pecans. Bake at 350° F. for 15–20 minutes.

Roast goose, garnished with winter squash, basil, thyme, and tomatoes

The following recipe, from Eliza Leslie's *Directions for Cookery in Its Various Branches* (31st ed., 1848), was used by archaeologist Daphne Derven when she prepared Christmas dinner 1850 style in Old City Park in Dallas, as described by *Texas Highways* in December 1984.

To Roast a Goose

"Having drawn and singed the goose, wipe out the inside with a cloth, and sprinkle in some pepper and salt. Make a stuffing of four good-sized onions minced fine and half their quantity of minced green sage leaves, a large tea-cupful of grated bread crumbs, a piece of butter the size of a walnut, and the beaten yolks of two eggs, with a little pepper and salt. Mix the whole together, and incorporate them well. Put the stuffing into the goose and press it in hard, but do not entirely fill up the cavity, because the mixture will swell in cooking. Tie the goose securely round with a greased or wetted string, and paper the breast to prevent it from scorching.

"Fasten the goose on the spit at both ends in the tin oven and put the oven in the fireplace. The fire must be brisk and well kept up. It will require from two hours to two and a half to roast. Baste it at first with a little salt and water, and then with its own gravy. Take off the paper when the goose is about half done, and dredge it with a little flour towards the last. Having parboiled the liver and heart, chop them and put them into the gravy, which must be skimmed well and thickened with a little browned flour.

"Send applesauce to table with the goose, also mashed potatoes. A goose may be stuffed entirely with potatoes, boiled and mashed with milk, butter, pepper, and salt. You may make a gravy of the giblets, that is the neck, pinions, liver, heart, and gizzard stewed in a little water, thickened with butter rolled in flour, and seasoned with pepper and salt. Add a glass of red wine. Before you send it to table, take out all but the liver and heart; mince them and leave them in the gravy. This gravy is by many preferred to that which comes from the goose in roasting. It is well to have both.

"If a goose is old it is useless to cook it, as when hard and tough it cannot be eaten."

Jessie Fantroy cooked for President and Mrs. Lyndon B. Johnson from 1953 to 1967. She says, "I don't cook fancy. My specialty is plain, old-fashioned food and plenty of it." Since 1973, she has cooked for employees and guests of a bank in Rio Vista, and they seem to like her cooking as much as the President did. Farther on, you'll find her recipes for vegetables, cobbler, and hot wassail, but let's start with a dish which has made a hit with foreign heads of state as well as a President's family.

Down Home Chicken and Dumplings

Chicken

1 3-pound fryer
2 quarts cold water or chicken stock
1 tablespoon salt
1 teaspoon pepper

Cook chicken until tender; remove from stove and let cool. Remove meat from bone and cut in 2- to 3-inch pieces.

Dumplings

6 cups flour
½ teaspoon baking powder
1 teaspoon salt
2 tablespoons shortening
¼ cup milk
1 cup water
1 egg, lightly beaten

Mix 3 cups flour, baking powder, salt, and shortening together. Add milk, water, and egg. This will make a sticky paste. Turn out on a floured board and knead in remaining flour until it becomes a large ball. Divide into small balls. Roll out thin (⅛ inch). Cut into strips 3 inches long.

Heat stock to a rolling boil, drop strips into stock, and put lid on pot. Turn off heat and leave covered for 25 minutes (no peeking, or dumplings will be gooey). Add chicken pieces to the pot. Do not stir, but shake the pot. Makes 6–8 generous servings.

In 1870, the first Chinese crew of 300 workers came to Calvert to build a railroad to Dallas. When the work was done, some of the laborers settled in towns along the route. Later, more Chinese came and stayed to farm. In several waves of immigration, subsequent groups opened small business stands or shops, or laundries, or restaurants.

Now Oriental immigrants come straight to the big cities. Jennifer H. McDowell looked into Houston's Chinatown in 1982 to find that Houston had become a magnet for Orientals.

"In Houston's Chinatown you won't find armadillo hatpins or designer jeans or chili for sale," she wrote. "However, if you're looking for an odd Chinese book, Oriental dolls or dishes, or for embroidered cloth shoes, brocade jackets and silk kimonos, rice wine and red bean pastries, a good Chinese buffet or a bone crushing kung fu movie, then you're in the right place."

Banquets play an especially significant role in traditional celebrations, like the Chinese Lunar New Year. But with the Chinese Texan community, and thousands of other Texans, any time is the right time for this old favorite from the U.T. Institute of Texan Cultures:

Chicken with Snow Peas, Water Chestnuts, and Bamboo Shoots

1 pound snow peas
2 tablespoons vegetable oil
½ teaspoon salt
1 cup uncooked boneless breast of chicken, in 1-inch pieces
½ cup bamboo shoots, sliced ¼ inch thick
½ cup water chestnuts, sliced
1 teaspoon soy sauce
⅓ cup chicken stock
2 teaspoons cornstarch
2 teaspoons water

Wash and drain snow peas, removing tips and strings. In a preheated skillet or wok place vegetable oil and salt. Bring oil to the sizzling point. Add chicken. Toss and turn rapidly at high heat for 1 minute. Add snow peas, bamboo shoots, water chestnuts, and soy sauce. Toss at high heat for 1 minute. Add chicken stock. Cover and cook for 2 minutes. Make a paste of cornstarch and water. Gradually add cornstarch paste to chicken mixture. Toss at high heat until sauce thickens.

We can't keep our fingers out of Louisiana's way with the East Texas fish and fowl. This one is special fare, borrowed from Fran Gerling's uncle, who lives in Port Arthur, Texas.

Clarence DeCoux's Wild Duck Gumbo

¾ cup oil
¾ cup flour
1 onion, finely chopped
2 stalks celery, finely minced
3 quarts water
1½ teaspoons salt
½ teaspoon black pepper
¼ teaspoon cayenne pepper
3 wild ducks, dressed
2 teaspoons gumbo filé powder

Heat oil in large Dutch oven. Add flour to oil and stir until it becomes a caramel brown color. Sauté onion and celery in this *roux*. Add water, salt, pepper, cayenne, and then the ducks. Bring the gumbo to a boil; lower heat and simmer 2½ hours. Adjust seasoning. Sprinkle gumbo filé powder over gumbo just before serving over mounds of Texas rice. If you do not wish to serve the gumbo with the ducks whole, then lift them out when they are done, allow to cool, and bone them. Reheat in the gumbo before serving. Gumbo can also be made with chicken or turkey.

A couple of good ideas from the magazine and the Texas Department of Agriculture:

Picnic Peanut Chicken

¾ cup flour
salt and pepper to taste
1 fryer, cut up
1 egg
1 cup orange marmalade
1 teaspoon dry mustard
2 cloves garlic
1½ cups peanuts, ground

Place flour, salt, and pepper in bag; add chicken, one piece at a time; shake to coat. Dip pieces in mixture of egg, marmalade, mustard, and garlic. Roll in peanuts. Bake at 375° F. about 40 minutes, until tender.

Kiss the holidays good-bye with this one:

Hot Turkey Salad

1 cup cooked turkey, cubed
1 cup chopped celery
2 cups chopped Texas pecans
½ cup mayonnaise
1 tablespoon lemon juice
1 tablespoon chopped onion
½ cup grated Cheddar cheese
salt and pepper to taste
crushed potato chips

Mix all ingredients except chips and place in a greased baking dish. Cover top with the chips. Bake at 350° F. about 30 minutes. Serves 4–6.

Eggs

Several years ago, *Texas High-ways* photographer Bob Parvin found Oma Koock's in Fredericksburg, tucked away in an old farm machinery building—". . . something akin to an 1850s German fellowship hall, a western saloon, a vaudeville stage, a hunter's lodge and an Old World restaurant." Even the town sheriff sat in on the band, law-and-order willing, to provide the oompah with his parade-scarred tuba.

TDA

Proprietor Guich Koock shared these recipes:

Hangtown Fry (Oyster Omelet)

8-ounce can of oysters
1 cup flour, seasoned with salt and
    pepper
4 tablespoons butter
6 eggs
2 tablespoons cream
4 tablespoons drawn butter
6 strips bacon, fried crisp

Drain oysters, dredge in seasoned flour, fry crisp in butter and remove from heat, but keep warm in a covered dish or warm oven. Beat eggs with cream. Add drawn butter to heated (not too hot) omelet pan and pour in beaten eggs. To allow eggs to coagulate evenly, lift from the bottom of the pan. Spread oysters across the top, flip omelet to let oysters settle in, then reverse so oyster layer faces up. Place in a warmed dish, add bacon strips across top and serve with German fried potatoes or peeled and sliced tomatoes. Serves 3.

Guich's Hill Country Quiche

3 eggs, beaten
1 cup half-and-half cream
¼ teaspoon dry mustard
½ teaspoon salt
pinch of nutmeg
½ cup thinly sliced jerky
1¼ cups grated Swiss cheese
9-inch pie shell

Mix ingredients in order given. Pour into pie shell and bake at 350° F. for about 45–60 minutes. If jerky is a bit salty, parboil it for a few minutes in 2 cups of water. Makes 4–6 servings.

A recent influx of chefs into Texas from abroad has stirred interest in grooming our own masters of *haute cuisine,* such as Richard Chamberlain, at Ratcliffe's in Dallas. Richard began studying culinary arts at El Centro College, then worked with superchef Dean Fearing at the Mansion on Turtle Creek as well as California's near-legendary Wolfgang Puck. One of Richard's innovative recipes combines crabmeat and corn in an egg custard.

Ratcliffe's Custard

1 cup fresh lump crabmeat
6 ears of corn, fresh or frozen
5 extra large eggs
1 pint cream
1 teaspoon salt, or to taste
½ teaspoon white pepper, or to taste

Heat oven to 350° F. Butter twelve 3-inch soufflé dishes or timbale molds (but not one big one). Carefully check crabmeat for shell bits and remove them.

To prepare corn: If fresh corn is used, remove from cob with knife and blanch for 2 minutes in boiling water; if frozen corn is used, allow it to thaw, but do not cook it.

Beat eggs, with either a wire whisk or an electric mixer; add cream, salt, and pepper, and continue beating until well blended. Fold in corn and crabmeat, and spoon mixture into soufflé dishes. Set dishes in a hot-water bath (about 1 inch deep). Place a single sheet of foil loosely over top of pan to prevent excessive browning. Bake 30 minutes or until firm on top.

To serve, loosen edges with a sharp knife and turn mold onto serving plate. Serves 12.

Improvisers will appreciate one of my favorite egg dishes for brunch or cocktail snacks. The original recipe demands only Cheddar cheese and artichoke hearts. I prefer Swiss cheese and add shredded, boiled ham and/or chopped mushroom pieces. Try it with your own favorite touches and seasonings.

Artichoked Eggs

2 tablespoons salad oil
2 tablespoons lemon juice
1 bunch green onions, minced, using
    the white and the lower part of the
    green tops
2 cloves garlic, minced
14-ounce can artichoke hearts,
    drained and cut into quarters
4 extra large eggs
½ teaspoon dry mustard
1 teaspoon salt
¼ teaspoon cayenne pepper
2 cups (8 ounces) Swiss or Cheddar
    cheese, grated
½ cup shredded boiled ham slices
2 ounce can mushroom pieces,
    drained
½ cup rolled cracker crumbs

Preheat oven to 350° F. and grease a 9-inch square pan. Heat salad oil and lemon juice in a skillet. Sauté the onions and garlic; remove from pan and set aside. Sauté artichoke hearts in the same pan. Beat eggs in a large bowl with mustard, salt, and cayenne pepper. Fold in artichokes, grated cheese, ham, and mushrooms. Stir in cracker crumbs and spread mixture in prepared pan. Bake for 40 minutes. Cut into 2-inch squares and serve hot, either with plates and forks or on toothpicks.

The Chicken-Fried Steak Summit— May 1983

Creative things can't always be reduced to measurements. Chicken-fried steak must be carefully pondered, then recited like poetry. When controversy arises, pitting the traditional preparation (such as *Texas Highways* editor Frank Lively's mama made in West Texas) against the new-fangled cracker-crumbs-and-buttermilk of gourmet authority David Wade, some highly qualified judge must be called in to monitor and summarize the debate. Mary Faulk Koock, restaurateur and cookbook author, arbitrates.

© Mike Flahive

Editor Lively begins:

Verna Lively's Chicken-Fried Steak

"She beat an egg into a bowl of milk, dipped a serving-size piece of round steak (which had the bejabbers pounded out of it) into the liquid, and then rolled the meat in flour that had been liberally laced with salt and pepper. Then she dropped it in hot grease about an inch deep. When the steak was cooked to a golden brown on both sides, she'd lift it out and place it on a paper sack . . .

"For the cream gravy, she'd pour off most of the grease, leaving a little with the browned drippings from the steak. She'd add 'just enough flour' to the pan and brown that for a few minutes before she added milk, and salt and pepper, of course. That gravy was almost as good as the CFS."

Of course, you had to have mashed (not whipped) potatoes, adds Lively, and maybe some green beans, and homemade hot rolls dripping with homemade butter.

Unless, of course, the chicken-fried steak was for breakfast, says the arbitrator:

Austin-Style Chicken-Fried Steak

"Mama simply trimmed the round steak, which had been delivered from Mr. Pate's market at 6:30 that very morning, cut it into serving pieces and hit each piece with the meat mallet on both sides to flatten slightly," says Mary Koock, who established Austin's Green Pastures restaurant. "She next dipped it into a shallow pan of flour seasoned with salt and pepper, and after shaking off all excess flour, placed it in the heavy iron skillet where about four tablespoons of hot shortening sizzled. She browned it on both sides, turning it only once, removed it to a large warm platter, and made cream gravy with the drippings left in the skillet . . .

"Never did we dream then that we were eating what was destined to become Texas' number one entree."

The chicken-fried steak recipe came with the house when Gaylann Stroth bought Convict Hill Restaurant, a popular restaurant at Oak Hill, close to Austin. This is it:

Convict Hill Chicken-Fried Steak

"Convict Hill uses top round steak for this dish, and seems to cook it in the traditional way: Two dips each into an egg and milk mixture, alternating with two into the seasoned flour, and then into the deep, hot oil fryer." Admittedly, a secret ingredient in the cream gravy and possibly one in the seasoned flour make the steak superbly delicious, says Mary Koock.

"Every cook adds his own technique in cooking and his own touch of seasoning to chicken-fried steak," she continues. "The basic differences are limited to whether the meat is pan fried or deep fat fried, the number of times the meat is dipped into batter or into seasoned flour or crumbs, and whether the cream gravy is served under or over on the side. But to make chicken-fried authentic, cream gravy is essential".

Approximately 90 percent of the 4,000 members of the Texas Restaurant Association, and possibly the same number of non-members, offer the delicacy. The association calculates that approximately 800,000 chicken-fried steaks are served every day in the Lone Star State.

C.A.'s Restaurant in Hurst, for instance, serves some 600 a day, each of them resting *on* the cream gravy and flanked by corn on the cob and fried okra.

A version made with cracker crumbs rather than flour is offered by television personality and author David Wade:

David Wade's Chicken-Fried Steak

"Trim fat off round steak, and cut in serving pieces. Lightly pound. Marinate in fresh buttermilk. Pulverize Ritz crackers; add seasoned salt, pepper, dry mustard, and a pinch or two of garlic powder to crumbs. Heat one-half inch vegetable oil in a heavy skillet to 360 degrees. Drain off milk, dip pieces of steak into the seasoned cracker crumbs, and place in the heated oil. Brown on each side, turning only once. Serve with cream gravy and mashed potatoes."

"Wade said it is important to have meat and coating the same temperature," wrote Mary Koock. "This prevents the coating from falling off. After steaks are coated with crumbs, place on a tray in the freezer for 5 or 10 minutes before frying in the hot oil."

Way back when the chuck wagon was the working cowboy's home on wheels, tidy packages of thinly sliced round steak weren't available on the range. The wagon carried neither freezer nor refrigeration, and beef was preserved on the hoof until slaughtered for meals. Then, after a selection of variety cuts were simmered to make "son-of-a-gun stew," the rest was cooled, wrapped in a tarp, and hung on the side of the wagon.

If you don't mind the heat, but want to get out of the kitchen anyway, the following camper's recipe for chicken-fried steak is straight off the chuck wagon. This recipe was made public at Abilene's International Cowboy Campfire Cookoffs in the 1970s. Its revelation, among other cowboy favorites, came from real chuck wagon cooks, Richard Bolt and John White. You can make this CFS at home, if you want to . . . who's ever going to know?

Chuck Wagon Chicken-Fried Steak (serves 4–6 cowboys)

Cut 2 pounds round steak into serving-size pieces and pound with a steak hammer or the butt end of a bottle until the tissues of the meat are broken. Mix 2 teaspoons salt and 2 teaspoons vinegar in a pan of cold water. Soak steak in the liquid 2 hours. Dredge each piece of steak in a mixture of 2 cups flour and 1 teaspoon black pepper. Fry in a skillet of deep hot cooking oil or grease. Fry until tender and brown on both sides. Keep steak warm while you make cream gravy: Allow excess brown flour to settle on the bottom of the skillet; pour off grease, leaving about 4 tablespoons in the skillet with the browned flour. Stir in about 2 heaping tablespoons flour; mix and brown. Place over fire; add 2 cups milk. Stir until gravy thickens and boils. Add salt and pepper to taste. "Anytime a chuck wagon cook serves chicken-fried steak without the cream gravy, he is in deep trouble," says Richard Bolt.

Cream Gravy

"Into approximately 2 tablespoons of pan drippings (or butter) add 2 level tablespoons of flour. Let it simmer over low heat three or four minutes without browning. Heat 2 cups of whole milk or half and half, and add to flour. Stir with a small wire whisk to prevent lumping. Continue stirring over heat until it thickens. Season to taste with salt and pepper. Add extra cream for thinner textures."

The envelope, please? Mary Koock concludes:

"The former mayor of Lamesa once observed that the worst chicken-fried steak he ever had was wonderful! In fact, a favorite saying among Texas newspaper columnists and other chicken fried steak lovers is that there are only three kinds . . . good, better, and whooooeeee!"

TTDA

Barbecue

When a Texan suggests, "Y'all come over for barbecue," listen carefully. The invitation might mean a brisket smoked on the back-yard grill, but it could easily mean a political affair for hundreds. Barbecue-minded hosts initiate the celebration of a wedding, graduation, or any occasion with a smoking wood or charcoal fire. Barbecue and smoke itself are celebrated at lunch counters every day.

Greg Whi

Barbecue can mean beef ribs, brisket, or sausage.

In February 1984, *Texas Highways* Managing Editor Tommie Pinkard reported that professional barbecuers actually stake their reputations on the particular flavor of their meat according to the kind of hard wood they use for smoke. Ed Dozier of Fulshear, outside of Houston, serves nothing but corn-fed beef, about 4,000 pounds of meat per week . . . all cooked over pecan wood.

"In a big smoker he designed in such a way that he can fine-tune the temperature, he cooks briskets seven or eight hours after rubbing them with paprika, salt and pepper. While they are cooking," wrote Tommie, "he mops them with a mixture of one part cooking oil to eight parts vinegar." But no sauce, unless it's served on the side.

Edgar A. (Smitty) Schmidt of Lockhart points out in the same article, "Good meat is the main thing in getting good barbecue, and I prefer to cook the clod, the top of the shoulder."

Smitty knows whereof he speaks: He has owned the Kreuz Market, a butcher shop, since 1948. He started smoking barbecue for sandwiches in a back room. Fire pits at one end of each of his brick smokers burn post oak, and the smoke is drawn over the meat by a big flue.

Some professionals insist on hickory; others prefer mesquite, post oak, or pecan wood. At home, at least, anything goes, except using barbecue sauce for basting. If used before the very last, it causes the meat to burn.

Surefire Barbecue

4-pound brisket, untrimmed
2 teaspoons black pepper
1 teaspoon red pepper
1 teaspoon onion salt
½ teaspoon dry mustard
2 tablespoons salt

Serious home barbecuers may begin by building a charcoal fire at one end of the grill. Cover 6 cups mesquite chips with water and soak for 1 hour.

Season brisket, except for the salt. Sear meat over white-hot coals 5 minutes on each side. Move brisket over to one side and spread 4 cups of the mesquite chips over the coals. With the grill covered, smoke brisket for 1 hour. Add salt to brisket, pour remaining mesquite chips on coals, and smoke for another hour, sprinkling water over chips, if necessary.

When the brisket has absorbed the smoky flavor, place in a baking pan, covered with heavy foil, and bake in a 200° F. oven for about 8 hours. Slice brisket across the grain and serve at once. Serves 10.

———————————————

Make barbecue sauce to be served separately:

Barbecue Sauce #1

½ cup melted fat from barbecued meat
1½ cups catsup
½ cup Worcestershire sauce
½ cup fresh lemon juice
⅓ cup brown sugar
⅓ cup chopped onion
⅓ cup water
hot pepper sauce to taste

Drain melted fat from barbecue pan into a saucepan. Add catsup, Worcestershire sauce, and lemon juice. Place over low heat and stir in other ingredients.

Good advice from an old pro came to *Texas Highways* recommended as an accompaniment to a holiday gift from the kitchen. Along with a whole brisket or a whole fresh ham . . .

"Fill two attractive sauce containers with a divided sauce to accompany it. Make one quart sour and piquant, for basting, and one quart of the same sauce with additional ingredients added for a thicker, richer, sweeter sauce. The recipe given here comes from an old, respected (but anonymous) commercial barbecue place.

"'Never add salt to basting sauce,' advises the source; 'it toughens the meat. Once the meat is nearly cooked, salt and mustard, other seasonings, and tomato sauce can be brought into the same base.'"

Barbecue Sauce #2

3 pints water
1 pint white distilled vinegar
1 heaping teaspoon black pepper, medium grind
1 heaping teaspoon ground red pepper (cayenne)
1 ground chile pepper or 1 tablespoon chili powder

Bring ingredients to a boil. Use half as a basting sauce. To the other half, add the following, and serve with the meat.

1½ cups catsup
¾–1 cup sugar
2 ounces Worcestershire sauce
1 tablespoon salt, or to taste

More Beef and Other Meats

The French have left cultural footprints all over Texas, bringing European knowledge and craftsmanship. In 1980, a new Hyatt Regency Hotel, the refurbished old Union Terminal building, and a glittering dandelion atop the adjacent Reunion Tower created a new Dallas landmark. *Texas Highways'* Tommie Pinkard saluted the French who established La Reunion community near the same spot in 1855. She wrote:

"La Reunion . . . a French-speaking community of intellectuals and craftsmen who came to Dallas and tried to be farmers in an area that was fit only to be a cement plant." They didn't get a single break with land or weather, and those who could afford to return to Europe did.

"The La Reunion exes brought to the rustic settlement named Dallas a cosmopolitan and urbane air unique for the time and region. So, along with general stores and saddlemakers, Dallas had in the late 1850s two private schools, a photographer, a cabinetmaker, a milliner, and a French tailor." There may have been a few chefs and restaurateurs. In any case, today the demand for French cuisine is strong in major Texas cities.

Jack Lewis

Texas Longhorn on the YO Ranch near Kerrville

In the past few years, the introduction of *la nouvelle cuisine* to Texas beef has produced some glorious combinations. Credit the following recipe, as served in La Reserve at Inn on the Park in Houston, to Executive Chef Ludger Szmania.

Harlequin of Beef

24 ounces beef tenderloin, center cut
8 ounces veal tenderloin
kosher salt
white pepper, freshly ground
1 ounce shallots, peeled and chopped
4 ounces red wine
½ teaspoon fresh thyme
1 bay leaf
½ teaspoon whole black peppercorns, crushed
16 ounces demi-glaze (reduced veal stock)
2 ounces butter

Note: Stock reduction is an essential part of professional French cuisine. At home, if veal stock is not available, use 2 cups of concentrated chicken stock or a 10¾-ounce can of undiluted consommé.

Remove fat and silver skin from beef and veal tenderloin. Season the veal with salt and white pepper and place in center of beef tenderloin. You do this by cutting gently with a knife into the center of the tender filet and working veal into place. Season the beef with salt and white pepper and tie with butcher's twine.

Sauté shallots lightly for a few minutes; deglaze with red wine and add thyme, bay leaf, and crushed peppercorns. Reduce by half and add demiglaze. Reduce by half again. Strain through chinoise or cheesecloth. Adjust seasoning, and finish with butter.

Sear the tenderloin in hot oil on all sides to color; finish in a 400° F. oven, 15–20 minutes for rare, or longer to individual taste. Let the meat stand for 5 minutes, remove the string, and slice. Arrange the meat on hot plates and pour sauce over it. Serves 4.

Texas farmers owe something to Cleng Peerson for steering the first Norwegian immigrant group to the Norse Belt of Bosque County, beginning in 1850. These sturdy Viking pioneers knew how to make the earth produce with a plow and oxen, and were grateful for the land they found around what is now Norse, Clifton, and Cranfills Gap. Then Ole Ringness simplified farming with an early version of the disc plow, later improved and patented by J. I. Case Company.

Saint Olav's, the old rock church, still stands at Norse, where the early Norwegian Texans worshiped in 1886. Now community activities, such as the Septemberfest and the December lutefisk dinner, are centered around the church and school at Cranfills Gap.

Leave lutefisk (pickled Norwegian cod) preparation to those who know how to do it; try, instead, this farmers' stew from *The Melting Pot*, the collection of ethnic recipes from the U.T. Institute of Texan Cultures.

Norwegian Goulash (Lapskaus)

2 pounds beef stew meat, cut up fine
½ pound lean salt pork, cut up
(¼ cup vegetable oil, if necessary)
1½ cups chopped celery
2 white onions, chopped
4 medium potatoes, diced or sliced
4 carrots, sliced (optional)
salt and pepper to taste
2 tablespoons soy sauce (optional)
2⅔ cups boiling water
(flour, if necessary)

Brown the stew meat with the salt pork (if the pork has no fat, add ¼ cup oil), and add celery, onions, potatoes, and carrots. Add remaining ingredients. Let simmer 1 hour or until meat is tender. Never boil, only simmer. Thicken gravy with a little flour if it appears too watery. Serves 6–8.

Greek and Lebanese Texans use similar methods and recipes to skewer lamb or beef and cook it over charcoal or under the broiler. If you use beef tenderloin, remember that it cooks very quickly; watch it. The U.T. Institute of Texan Cultures offers the Greek version of Mrs. Irene Sockler, San Antonio:

Souflaki

3 pounds beef, lamb, or pork
1 cup olive oil
⅓ cup lemon juice
½ cup wine
salt and pepper
oregano
1 or 2 cloves garlic, chopped
2 or 3 bay leaves
3 medium onions, sliced thin
cherry tomatoes or quartered large ones
small onions or quartered medium ones
bell pepper, cut in 1-inch squares
mushroom caps (optional)

Cut meat into 1½-inch cubes. Combine olive oil, lemon juice, and wine. Pour this marinade over the meat, which has been placed in a large, shallow porcelain or oven-proof glass pan. Sprinkle with salt and pepper, oregano, and garlic. Add bay leaves and sliced onions. Weigh down with heavy plates, cover with foil, and refrigerate 5 hours or overnight.

Remove meat from marinade and skewer on wood or metal skewers, alternating with tomatoes, onions, pepper squares, and mushroom caps. Cook skewers over charcoal or in the kitchen broiler, basting and turning occasionally. Baste with marinade or melted butter. Cook for 25–30 minutes or until cooked to taste. Serve immediately. Makes 9–12 servings.

The combination of ethnic taste and Texan resourcefulness has produced many a casserole, such as the following Italian-influenced dish from the Imperial collection of oldies, slightly adapted to include seasoning and oil for sautéing.

You probably have most things on hand to do this one on any given week night. To make it even better, add 1 tablespoon mixed Italian herb seasoning and ½ teaspoon garlic salt to the listed ingredients.

Italian Hash

2 cups raw elbow macaroni
½ cup chopped onions
¼ cup chopped green pepper
2 tablespoons salad oil
1 pound lean ground meat
¾ cup grated cheese
1 cup canned tomatoes, chopped (with juice)
salt and pepper to taste

Cook macaroni according to package directions. Sauté onions and pepper in oil. Remove from oil; set aside. Brown meat in same pan. Stir meat into macaroni in a 2-quart baking dish, then stir in grated cheese.

Combine tomatoes with onions and pepper. Salt and pepper to taste. [Add Italian seasoning and garlic salt.] Pour tomato sauce over macaroni, meat, and cheese mixture. Top with additional cheese and bake about 30 minutes in 350° F. oven. Serves 6.

The Texas wine industry began at a Franciscan mission in El Paso in the seventeenth century, when Indian converts to Christianity celebrated the Eucharistic Feast with sacramental wine made from Mexican grapes. But it was 1970 before Texas producers started a movement to develop winemaking on a large scale.

By 1984, wine itself had become an occasion to celebrate. Just for *Texas Highways*, Sarah Jane English and Fran Gerling got Texas holiday-type recipes together to serve and make with Texas wine. Here's one winner:

Jack Lewis

Texas Wine Beef

5-pound chuck roast
Lawry's seasoned salt
garlic salt
½ pound bacon
3 or 4 large carrots, diced
4 cloves garlic, crushed
2 leeks, chopped
2 medium onions, chopped
½ cup parsley, minced
2½ cups Texas red wine
3 bay leaves
1 teaspoon thyme
½ cup fresh mushrooms, sliced (optional)
flour and water for thickening paste

Rub both sides of roast with seasoned salts; sear. Roast at 350° F. for 1½ hours. It should be crusty and well done. Cool and cube. Reserve drippings; add enough water for gravy. Set aside.

Fry bacon, and retain enough grease to cook vegetables. Drain bacon when crisp. Add carrots, garlic, leeks, onions, and parsley to bacon grease and cook slowly, stirring until the carrots look candied.

Place cubed meat in heavy casserole, and cover with the wine. Add bay leaves, thyme, and pan drippings. Add cooked vegetables and place in a moderate oven (350° F.) about 2 hours. Add bacon and fresh mushrooms (optional) for last few minutes. The sauce should be thick, not watery. Correct with flour paste if necessary. Serve on wild rice, if available. Makes 6 large or 8 small servings.

Serve Cypress Valley red table wine or Llano Estacado Cabernet Sauvignon.

Note: This dish may be prepared a week in advance and frozen.

The Texas Rice Council has ways of making East Texas long grain rice even better. The council gave this recipe to *Texas Highways*. Try it, when you want to extend 1½ pounds of round steak to 6 servings. When it's for company, add class by using thin slices of tenderloin, if you can, or sirloin, and don't cook it so long.

Beef Bavarian

1½ pounds beef round steak, sliced as thinly as possible
2 tablespoons cornstarch
2 teaspoons salt
¼ teaspoon pepper
¼ teaspoon garlic powder
2 tablespoons vegetable oil
1 large onion, sliced
12-ounce can beer
1 cup beef broth
¼ teaspoon Tabasco pepper sauce
1 tablespoon brown sugar
4 large carrots, sliced
3 cups hot cooked rice

Have butcher tenderize steak, or pound it until thin. Cut into 1-inch-wide strips. Blend cornstarch, salt, pepper, and garlic powder, and coat meat with the mixture. Brown in oil. Add onion; cook 2 or 3 minutes longer. Stir in beer, broth, pepper sauce, and brown sugar. Bring to a boil, reduce heat, cover, and simmer 15 minutes. Add carrots and cook 15 minutes longer or until meat is tender. Spoon over beds of fluffy rice. Makes 6 servings.

Texas Highways recommended this one for a different treatment to a holiday ham. Have it with the Texas wine you get for Christmas.

Sweet and Sour Holiday Ham

⅓ cup chopped Bermuda onion
⅓ cup chopped green onion
1 cup chopped sweet bell pepper (red or green)
1 cup celery
2 tablespoons butter
1½ tablespoons each flour and butter for paste
1 can apricot nectar (12 ounces)
1 teaspoon prepared mustard
1 tablespoon white wine vinegar
¼ cup catsup
¼ cup apricot preserves
salt and fresh cracked pepper to taste
2½ cups ham (cooked and diced or sliced)
4 cups cooked rice

Sauté onions, bell pepper, and celery in butter on low heat slowly for 5 minutes. Separately, melt second portion of butter and mix in flour for a paste. Add apricot nectar, mustard, vinegar, catsup, and preserves, and season with salt and fresh cracked pepper. Add onions, bell pepper, and celery to thickened nectar mixture. Stir until smooth. Add ham and heat thoroughly on low heat for 20 minutes. Serve on rice. If desired, reserve 2 tablespoons each of red bell pepper and celery for garnish. Choose Fall Creek Vineyards' Chenin Blanc or Val Verde Winery's Lenoir to complement this dish. Serves 5.

If you have been looking for a gourmet-class roast lamb entree for a spectacular dinner party, this is it . . . for two whole loins.

A rapid expansion of the luxury hotel and restaurant industry has brought an influx of superbly trained European chefs to Texas. Among them, the Adolphus Hotel's executive chef, Victor Gielisse, stands out as a habitual winner of international awards and medals. In 1984, Gielisse and Markus Bosiger, of Houston's Westin Hotel, were members of the USA Culinary Olympic Team. Both chefs won gold medals individually as well as the gold medal for the United States team's joint entry, below.

Roast Loin of Lamb

2 double loins of lamb, with trimmings (9 ounces each)
6 ounces fresh pork fat (thick and white)
4 egg whites
1 ounce pine nuts
1 tablespoon butter
1 shallot, minced
2 ounces shredded carrot
3 ounces spinach leaves
1 bunch scallions, sliced
½ cup chopped parsley
2 tablespoons mushrooms, finely chopped
3 cloves garlic
¼ teaspoon rubbed thyme
1 tablespoon kosher salt
½ teaspoon black pepper
½ teaspoon coriander
8 ounces caul fat (pork), sliced thin, for wrapping
salt and pepper to taste
lamb bones cut in small pieces
1 tablespoon fresh ginger, minced
dry red wine
espagnole sauce
1 cup butter

Bone whole loin roasts, reserving both loin and tenderloin sides (four pieces). Reserve bone for sauce. Dice all trimmed lean meat and pork fat, chill, and puree in food processor till smooth. Add egg whites one at a time till blended.

Prepare vegetables, saving scraps. While preparing the roast, place reserved bones and vegetable scraps in 350° F. oven till well browned.

Sauté pine nuts in 1 tablespoon butter. Add shallot, carrots, spinach, scallions, parsley, mushrooms, 2 cloves garlic, thyme, salt, pepper, and coriander. Stir over low heat until the liquid disappears. Chill in freezer and then blend into forcemeat.

Spread 2 sheets of caul fat on a flat surface. Divide forcemeat into 4 parts. Cover each sheet of fat with a thin layer of forcemeat. Lay the loin half down first; cover with forcemeat. Then lay the tenderloin on top. Wrap the caul fat up around the loins and tuck the ends beneath them. Sprinkle with salt and pepper and roast for 20 minutes at 375° F. Let rest 5 minutes before slicing.

To prepare sauce: Add ginger, 1 clove garlic, red wine, and espagnole sauce (or brown stock) to roasted bones and scraps. Cook 30 minutes, strain, and finish by whisking in 1 cup butter. Serves 8.

The Chinese Texan community has the best idea for pork tenderloin, this from the U.T. Institute of Texan Cultures:

Chinese Barbecued Pork

1 pound pork tenderloin
½ teaspoon monosodium glutamate
½ cup soy sauce
⅓ cup sugar
½ teaspoon garlic powder
2 tablespoons catsup
¼ teaspoon salt

Slice pork into two strips. Combine remaining ingredients. Add pork and marinate in the sauce for about 3 hours, turning frequently. Drain the pork and place it on an oven rack.

Roast at 350° F. for 45 minutes, turning every 10 minutes to assure even browning. Slice the pieces ¼ inch thick. Serves 4.

Beef Jerky

To say that Panhandle Texans take beef very seriously is like saying that South Texans remember the Alamo. Amarillo, with its ranching heritage, is also the center of feedlots, where cattle are brought to the precise weight and grade specifications of meat packers. Amarillo's Western Stockyards holds the largest cattle auction in the world.

Saddlebag staples: Hardtack and Beef Jerky

If you need a snack for your next trail ride, Amarillo home economist Lynn Howell's beef jerky recipes are updated versions of the historical "c" (for "cowboy") rations. Backpacking pedestrians sometimes like to snack on them, too. In one method, the meat is brushed with sauce; in the other recipe, the strips are marinated during the preparation.

Lynn's Beef Jerky

1 pound beef loin tip or beef brisket (ask butcher to slice paper thin)
Jetton's Barbecue Sauce (or another with no sugar)
onion salt
garlic salt

If necessary, roll out meat slices as thin as possible. Trim off fat. Set oven at 200° F. and line cookie sheets with foil. Brush one side of meat with sauce. Put slices on cookie sheet; *do not stack*. Sprinkle lightly with onion and garlic salts. Cook for 8–9 hours. Turn meat after 6 hours of cooking and brush with sauce. Cool and store in a tightly covered jar or sealed in a plastic bag.

© Tom Algire

Texas rainbow cactus in Big Bend National Park

Lynn's Marinated Beef Jerky

1 pound loin tip (or brisket, or flank), sliced paper thin
½ teaspoon pepper
1 teaspoon onion powder
½ teaspoon garlic salt
3 tablespoons plus 1 teaspoon soy sauce
5 tablespoons Worcestershire sauce

Trim all fat off the beef. Mix other ingredients together. Marinate meat overnight in the mixture. Remove from marinade and pat meat between paper towels. Line cookie sheet with foil and arrange meat on it in a single layer. Dry for 8 or more hours at 200° F., turning after 6 hours. Cool and store in a tightly covered jar or sealed in a plastic bag.

For the historically correct version of jerky, here's the oldie from *Texas Highways* contributor, outdoor cook, and writer Fayanne Teague. Serve with hardtack, if you have a mind (and the teeth, of course) to do it.

Original Jerky

Cut meat into strips ½ inch thick by 1 inch wide. String onto a piece of wire or cord. Dip into boiling brine solution (1 cup salt to 1 gallon water) until meat loses its red color. Remove meat from water and let drip dry. Hang near a fire, but not so close as to cook the meat. May be air dried or sun dried, but this takes much longer (days or weeks), and the meat must be protected from insects.

Fayanne's Modern Jerky

2 pounds round steak, 1 inch thick
½ cup Worcestershire sauce
1 teaspoon salt
pepper to taste
2 tablespoons parsley flakes
¼ teaspoon garlic powder (optional)

Note: Chili powder, barbecue salt, paprika, horseradish, and onion salt or flakes may also be used in the marinade.

Slice round steak into ½-inch wide strips and place in a single layer in a pan or baking dish. Mix other ingredients and pour over meat. Marinate in refrigerator overnight. Remove and place meat carefully on cookie sheet. Dry in 175° F. oven for 1 hour, and then reduce temperature to 150° F. Continue baking strips in the low oven until dry, but pliable, 1–3 hours. Cool jerky and store in tightly sealed containers.

3

Tex-Mex . . . and Mex-Tex

Jack Lewis

Tex-Mex

True devotees of Tex-Mex cuisine can go just so long without a big steaming pot of homemade tamales. This recipe for 15 dozen, from Flora Gonzales of Austin, feeds a big family gathering. Of course, the recipe can be halved, but since the tamales take a long time to prepare, it's worth your while to make the whole batch. Steam the number you need, and freeze the rest. They freeze well uncooked.

John Suhrstedt

Flora Gonzales of Austin prepares 18 dozen tamales at a time for family Christmas gatherings.

Gonzales Tamales

Shucks

Wash, remove corn silk, and trim ragged ends on 15 dozen corn shucks. Soak in water at least 20 minutes, or until flexible. Remove from water.

Meat Filling

4 pounds boneless pork
1 teaspoon powdered cumin
6 ounces chili powder
½ teaspoon garlic powder, or to taste
salt and pepper to taste

Simmer pork until tender, drain (save the broth), and cool. Chop or coarse grind, combine with spices, and stir filling over low heat until blended and warm.

Masa

5 pounds *masa harina*
¼ pound pure lard, melted
1 ounce chili powder
salt, to taste
pork broth

Mix ingredients, using just enough broth to make a soft dough that does not stick to the fingers.

Assembly

Place a heaping tablespoon of *masa* on the smooth side of the corn shuck, spread in a rectangle to top and side edges of the shuck. Spoon on a heaping tablespoon of meat filling. Fold one side to the center, then fold other side over to enclose filling. Fold up bottom end. Stand tamales, open end up, on a rack in a large pan. Pour in about 2 inches of water, cover tamales with foil and then with lid. Simmer about 45 minutes. If additional water is needed, pour in carefully at edge of pan.

Keep this one in mind for a quick casserole:

Chili and Hot Tamale Casserole

1 medium onion
2 tablespoons butter
15-ounce can chili, without beans
1 cup cooked rice
15-ounce can tamales
½ cup grated Cheddar cheese

Sauté onion in butter. Add chili and bring to boil. In a casserole, alternate layers of chili mixture with rice and tamales, ending with chili on top. Sprinkle with grated Cheddar cheese. Bake at 350° F. 30 minutes. Serves 3.

Nachos with Frijoles

12-ounce can refried beans
6 cups corn tortilla chips (plain Doritos or Tostitos)
2 cups grated Cheddar cheese
3-ounce can sliced jalapeños
1 cup chopped tomato
2 tablespoons minced onion

Heat refried beans in saucepan. Spread hot beans on each tortilla chip, and place on a shallow baking dish or heat-proof platter. Sprinkle with cheese and jalapeños. Bake at 400° F. for 5 minutes or until cheese melts. Remove from oven; sprinkle with tomato and onion. Makes 8 appetizer servings.

Note: This recipe lends itself to other cold toppings as well, such as guacamole and sour cream.

Guacamole

2 large ripe avocados
2 tablespoons lime juice
½ cup finely chopped onion
½ cup finely chopped fresh cilantro leaves
2 finely chopped jalapeño peppers
¾ cup cubed and drained ripe tomato
salt to taste

Cut avocados in half, remove seeds, and scoop out pulp with a spoon. Mash pulp with a fork into a soft puree. Add remaining ingredients, mixing well. Chill. Makes 3 cups.

Eggs with Mexican Sausage

6 chorizo sausages
1 dozen eggs, slightly beaten

Cut chorizo sausage into bite-size pieces. Fry until slightly brown. Add beaten eggs and scramble with sausages until done. Salt to taste. Serve with flour tortillas or skillet bread.

The Texas Department of Agriculture in 1985 used these recipes to show off the taste of Texas in New York:

Fajitas

2¼ pounds skirt steak, ¼ inch thick
1 tablespoon garlic salt
juice of 5 limes
¼ cup vegetable oil
steamed flour tortillas
picante sauce

Pound steak to ⅛-inch thickness. Sprinkle both sides with garlic salt and lime juice. Cover and refrigerate overnight. Drain well; discard marinade. Place steak on grill and cook over medium heat 8–10 minutes per side, occasionally brushing with oil. Remove from grill and cut into thin slices. Place meat on flour tortillas. Sprinkle with picante sauce. Wrap tortillas. Serves 6–8.

Fajitas in Beer Marinade

2 pounds skirt steak
salt and pepper
¼ cup vinegar
12-ounce can beer
juice of 2 fresh lemons

Season skirt steak with salt and pepper. Combine vinegar, beer, and lemon juice in a shallow pan. Place meat in pan and marinate 8–24 hours in refrigerator. Grill steak over coals (preferably with Texas mesquite chips). Serves 4.

Mex-Tex

For years, indigenous Tex-Mex dishes have been called "Mexican food." Nevertheless, neither Texans nor Mexicans have been deceived. Real Mexican food has crossed the border, and while it may take on some Tex-Mex appearances, it remains more Mexican than Texan. In the December 1981 issue, *Texas Highways* consulted food writer Maggi Stewart on assembling the traditional Mexican Christmas dinner, to be served after Midnight Mass.

"Keep in mind that Mexican cooks glory in unmeasure," advises Maggi, "following the adage, *no le hace*, it doesn't matter. Use the chiles (or other ingredients) as they come, to your taste.

"Start with the two basic sauces, red and green. They enliven the simplest dishes and are as imperative for the table setting as salt and pepper." And then, *moles* and *tingas* (Aztec and European type sauces). Of course, you will start your Christmas dinner with the Ensalada de Noche Buena (Holy Night Salad), and an aspic wreath of pickled beets.

Jack Lewis

Ensalada de Nopalitos combines tender young cactus with avocado slices and tomat

Ensalada de Noche Buena

"Line the bowl with lettuce, and arrange these colorful ingredients over it: thin slices of beets, oranges, apples, bananas, pineapple, and limes, decorated with chopped peanuts and seeds of two pomegranates. Some serve homemade mayonnaise, some French dressing. Originally, one-half cup sugar was mixed with three or four tablespoons wine vinegar to dress this special salad."

Wreathed Pickled Beets

1 package lemon gelatin
2 16-ounce cans sliced or diced beets, chopped fine
¼ cup honey
1½ cups vinegar
5 or 6 whole cloves

Prepare lemon gelatin using one-half the usual amount of water. When syrupy, add drained beets, honey, vinegar, and cloves. This amount will fill a 3-cup ring mold and make a pretty wreath. Serve in wedges.

Mole Poblano

8-pound turkey
6 ancho chiles
6 pesilla chiles
4 mulato chiles
2 onions, chopped
4 cloves garlic, chopped
½ teaspoon anise
4 tablespoons sesame seeds
2 or 3 sprigs cilantro
1 pound tomatoes
1 cup almonds
½ cup raisins
½ teaspoon ground cloves
½ teaspoon cinnamon
½ teaspoon cumin
4 tablespoons lard
1½ ounces unsweetened chocolate broken into pieces
salt and pepper to taste

Cut turkey into serving pieces and put in water to cover. Simmer 2 hours or until tender. Remove veins from chiles; discard veins. Probably in several small batches, blend chiles with next eleven ingredients. Heat lard to sizzle and add the puree, lowering heat quickly to avoid splattering. Stir constantly with wooden spoon for 5 minutes. Add 2 cups broth from simmering turkey pieces. Add chocolate and salt and pepper. Arrange turkey pieces in a casserole and cover with mole. Cover the casserole and simmer 30 minutes to blend flavors. Serves 8–10.

Tequila Soup

1 head cabbage, chopped coarse
2 green peppers, cut in strips
2 onions, chopped
1 bunch celery, chopped
6 garlic cloves, sliced
2 green chiles, deveined and diced
1 bay leaf
3 or 4 black peppercorns
3 or 4 white peppercorns
1 small bunch cilantro
salt to taste
tequila (approx. 1 cup)

Now this is a green health soup. You simply set on a clay pot of cold water (4 cups, or enough to cover the vegetables nicely), chop the vegetables chunky, dump everything in, and let it simmer . . . all 90 calories of it. Make it a day ahead, if possible. Blend the green vegetables, warm the soup, lace it with tequila to taste . . . about a cupful. Serves 12.

Mexican Chocolate

2 cups milk
1 ounce unsweetened chocolate plus 1 tablespoon sugar, ½ teaspoon cinnamon, and a pinch of salt
or
1 ounce prepared Mexican chocolate (half of a 2-ounce cake)

Combine ingredients in double boiler. Heat until chocolate melts. Beat until foamy and serve in cups. For drama, beat in a pitcher with a Mexican *molinillo*, a wooden beater, twirling the tool between your palms Aztec style. Or use an electric blender. If you have cinnamon sticks (*canela*), offer those to stir the individual cups. Makes 2 servings.

Avocado Tequila Cream

6 avocados, peeled and halved
2 tablespoons honey
½ cup lime juice
½ cup tequila
1 cup heavy cream, whipped
lime slices for garnish

Puree avocados with honey, lime juice, and tequila. Fold in whipped cream. Serve in compotes, garnished with lime slices. Serves 12.

The Mexican soup below came to *Texas Highways* as part of a January 1986 soup feature, from Fran Gerling. Confidentially, the soup is supposed to prevent or cure a hangover, and is often served after a night on the town, or perhaps the next morning. But *Texas Highways* wouldn't want to raise your hopes, so don't count on it.

Menudo

6 pounds tripe, cut in 1-inch pieces
1 gallon of water
2 medium onions, chopped
2 cloves garlic
1 tablespoon salt
½ teaspoon black pepper
2 ancho chiles
1 tablespoon fresh cilantro leaves
7 cups cooked hominy
lime wedges for garnish

Place tripe, water, onions, garlic, salt, and pepper in a large kettle and simmer over low heat for about 2 hours, skimming fat as necessary. Toast the chiles well. Slit them open and remove the seeds and veins. Grind them until they are very fine and add to the kettle. Add cilantro and simmer for another 2 hours. Add hominy and cook another 30 minutes. Serve with lime wedges. Serves 10–12.

Prickly pear (nopal) gets a lot of bad press for its spines and glochids (barbed hairs), but, in fact, the humble cactus enjoys a strong, but mixed following . . . or, at least, a public of sorts. The Coahuiltecan Indians dried the fruit like figs and pounded the skin into flour. Today, people like the young fruit breaded and fried, or added to omelets, or made into candy. *Ensalada de nopalitos*, or cactus salad, is another favorite, as is prickly pear jelly.

Other serious aficionados, however, take the cactus *au natural*. White-tailed deer depend on the barbed fare for about 30 percent of their annual diet. The javelina (collared peccary) demands enough for 60 percent of its diet, and if the cactus is plentiful, enough for 100 percent of the wild pig's water supply. For that matter, even cattle sometimes prefer prickly pear to grass, if the rancher caters by burning off the spines. Wild turkeys like the seeds; bees like the nectar.

Nearly everyone who has tried it describes picking the fruit (*tuna*) as "he-e-ell-laceous!" Still, they go looking for the red, ripe *tuna*, wearing thick leather gloves, if not a suit of armor, and pick the fruit with the longest tongs they can find. Then, holding the *tuna* on a long spear of some kind, they burn the stickers over a flame and scrape away the residue with a sharp knife. Even then, peeling the fruit requires rubber gloves, to prevent purple-dyed hands.

By the way, when you go out picking the fruit, watch out for snakes and wasps; they like it too.

Writer and photographer Frank Beesley, who researched the prickly pear for *Texas Highways*, May 1982, offers the solution:

If you aren't prepared to go through all that, just buy some of the prepared prickly pear products in highway specialty shops.

If you insist on making your own, try this recipe from Miguel Ravago of Austin's Fonda San Miguel, or cactus jelly (see p. 110).

Geoff Appold

Tequila Soup combines vegetables, herbs, and tequila.

Ensalada de Nopalitos

2 cups nopal cactus
2 medium tomatoes, chopped
3 tablespoons olive oil
4 teaspoons red wine vinegar
¼ teaspoon oregano
⅓ cup white onion, chopped fine
½ teaspoon salt
6 sprigs fresh cilantro
freshly ground pepper
lettuce and sliced avocado for garnish

Mix all ingredients in a large bowl, and set aside for about an hour. Before serving, garnish with lettuce and avocado slices.

Another bite of Mexico comes to friends of Dallas clothes designer Cristina Barboglio Lynch in the form of *salsa ranchera*, semi-prepared and delivered right away to friends especially fond of *huevos rancheros*. "But it's HOT," she warns, "so those who like a milder sauce add more tomatoes. But this recipe I got from my father in Mexico, so I make it his way":

Salsa Ranchera de La Barboglio

4 medium tomatoes
6 chiles (jalapeños)
½ clove garlic, minced
up to ⅓ cup water (if needed)

salt to taste
½ onion, diced
2 tablespoons vegetable oil

Peel tomatoes and chiles by dropping them in boiling water until their skins split. Remove skins from both tomatoes and chiles; then remove seeds and veins of the chiles. Mash tomatoes and chiles (use a *molcajete*, if you have one, or a mortar and pestle). While mashing, add garlic and salt. If the tomato mixture seems too pasty, add up to ⅓ cup water.

Store sauce at this stage in refrigerator until ready to use. If sauce is given at this point, supply instructions for completion: Sauté diced onion in vegetable oil until yellow and transparent. Add the tomato-chile mixture and cook until the mixture is hot, then remove from heat. Makes 2 servings.

Pack the sauce, semi-cooked or complete, in a cut-glass jar. Include the recipe for *huevos rancheros*, if you wish.

Huevos Rancheros

Fry 2 corn tortillas briefly in hot vegetable oil. Spread each tortilla with warmed *frijoles*, then top with a thin slice of fried ham. Fry an egg over-easy, or scramble, and place on the ham. Spoon hot *salsa ranchera* over all. Makes 2 servings.

More *Texas Highways salsas:*

Salsa Cruda

2 raw tomatoes, chopped fine
2 or more serrano chiles
1 onion chopped fine
1 tablespoon cilantro, chopped fine
salt and pepper
pinch of sugar

Mix ingredients and serve cold. Makes about 2½ cups.

Hot Sauce (Chile Macho)

24 jalapeño peppers
2 medium onions
8-ounce can tomato sauce
1 teaspoon salt

Chop peppers and onions. Add tomato sauce and salt. Ready to serve. Makes 4 cups.

Salsa Verde

10-ounce can Mexican green tomatoes, drained
1 small onion, chopped
2 or more canned serrano chiles, chopped
1 clove garlic, chopped
6 sprigs fresh cilantro, chopped
salt and pepper

Blend ingredients. Adjust seasonings. Makes about 1½ cups.

Note: If you use fresh *tomatillos* (green tomatoes), you must cook them until soft, about 10 minutes. Then add other ingredients.

Randy Green

4

Chili

TDA

Chili

Whenever you want to start an argument, count on chili, which probably ranks third after religion and politics on the all-time list of unresolved arguments. While some Texans measure the quality of taste according to a particular commercial seasoning mix, purists might grind several kinds of peppers with the same number cloves of garlic, add fresh tomatoes, beer, cilantro, mole, and other special ingredients, and insist that the sacred feast be prepared in an iron pot. Every cook can find or invent a suitable recipe in the spectrum of Texas chili, ranging from a mild tomato sauce to a single degree below spontaneous combustion. Moreover, Displaced-Yankee chili may have not only more tomatoes than zip, but also *noodles*.

In a March 1979 review of the various aspects of the Brimstone Brew, *Texas Highways'* Tommie Pinkard determined that, while all agree that chili is the perfect state dish, the definition of real chili depends on the interpreter's taste buds. Her case rests on some interesting folkloric trivia:

When H. Allen Smith declared Texas chili a religion rather than a comestible in a 1966 *Holiday* magazine article, he was reaching for humor, but he touched something closer to truth. He wasn't the first to make the observation. In *With or Without Beans* (1952), Joe E. Cooper wrote, "In Texas four things temporal are held inviolate . . . women, states' rights, cattle brands, and chili."

For all the religious significance humorists direct toward celebration of the *Capsicum frutescens*, nobody has identified the inspired Texan who first threw chiles into a simmering pot of beef. One theory credits transplanted Canary Islanders in San Antonio with inventing chili around 1731, when they attempted to find a spicy substitute for curry flavor. Other signs point to early cowboys, livening up the taste of their stringy, tough Longhorn beef.

In any case, the dish began gaining universal popularity in 1882, when the so-called chili queens of San Antonio stirred up vats of the succulent stew to sell on the street. Powdered formulas patented by William Gebhardt and Dewitt Clinton Pendery made chili a household word in the 1890s. By 1910, even those who didn't make chili could buy it in cans, and before the end of the 1970s, canned chili sales had approached $200 million a year.

Meanwhile, newspaperman Wick Fowler had brought a further refinement to the powdered formula idea by sealing separately bagged ingredients into packages with directions for 1-Alarm, 2-Alarm, and False-Alarm chili. That innovative development stirred interest in still more chili pots when Fowler was pitted against H. Allen Smith at the first Terlingua Cookoff in 1967. Although the result was a tie, enthusiasm for the event made it a landmark in the history of chili. Now chili has become anybody's game, and cookoffs come up on a regular basis in all parts of Texas.

At Terlingua, unusual additions may have some merit. Winners of the championship cookoff sometimes add sausage or bacon or, possibly, farkleberries, rattlesnake, or armadillo. The late Frank X. Tolbert, founder of the cookoff, really liked it HOT. He directed his own expertise to an appreciative following in a newspaper column, two books, and his Chili Parlor restaurants.

Most people, however, seem to lean toward a balance of flavors, rather than one overpowering substance. Still, critical questions must be decided: Onions and tomatoes or not? Well, then, what about beans?

Hunters returning with their quota of venison usually have their own special recipes for chili. Adding beef suet to the ground venison offsets the dryness of the meat. Wick Fowler's 2-Alarm mixture, applied according to package directions, covers the salty flavor of venison. Still, Texans who made chili before the balanced spice package was marketed like to make it from scratch.

J. Griffis Smith

However you prefer your brimstone brew, keep a firm hold on the spiritual significance of chili with this chili-eaters' prayer ending, composed by old-time Panhandle range cook Matthew "Bones" Hooks:

"Chili eaters is some of Your chosen people. We don't know why You are so doggone good to us. But, Lord God, don't ever think we ain't grateful for this chili we are about to eat. Amen."

In the spring of 1977, after a record-breaking chili party at Austin's Zilker Park that featured 2,300 pounds of beef, 100 pounds of spices, and a green garden hose full of water, Representatives Ron Bird of San Antonio and Ben Grant of Marshall saw their resolution passed in the Texas House of Representatives and Senate, and chili was declared the official dish of the State of Texas.

Texas Highways featured Bird's recipe for "gringo chili" along with Frank Tolbert's "bowl of red" and Mrs. Lyndon B. Johnson's "Pedernales River chili." My recipe is included for those who reject onions and tomatoes, but add separately cooked beans. I call it "Texas-OU Chili Pot" after my favorite fall occasion to make it.

Frank Tolbert's Bowl of Red

6–9 ancho chile pods
3 pounds lean chuck, in bite-size or coarse ground pieces
cooking oil
2 ounces rendered beef kidney suet, if desired
1 tablespoon ground oregano
1 tablespoon ground cumin seed
1 tablespoon salt
1 tablespoon (or less) powdered cayenne pepper
1 tablespoon Tabasco sauce
2 cloves (or more, to taste) garlic, minced
2 heaping tablespoons *masa harina* (or cornmeal)

Prepare chiles: Wash and remove stems and seeds (wear rubber gloves and don't touch your eyes); boil 30 minutes until skins will slip off. Chop or grind. Save the water to add to the meat.

Sear the meat in a small amount of cooking oil, and put it in a big pot with the suet, peppers, and enough liquid to cover the meat. Simmer 30 minutes. Add the rest of the ingredients, except *masa*, and simmer another 45 minutes. Add more water as needed. Skim grease, if any, and mix in *masa*. Cook another 30 minutes and taste for seasoning. Add more chile peppers if desired. To remove all fat, chill. The fat will solidify on top where it can be easily removed. A heaping tablespoon of chili powder can be substituted for each chile pod. Serves 8.

Ron Bird's Gringo Chili

1 pound lean ground chuck
1 large onion, diced
2 cloves garlic, chopped fine, or 1 teaspoon ground garlic
salt to taste
1 tablespoon bacon drippings
15½-ounce can whole tomatoes, chopped
2 ounces chili powder
1 ounce cumin seed, crushed
¼ teaspoon ground oregano
6-ounce can tomato sauce or equivalent amount of catsup
1 cup water

Combine meat, onion, garlic, and salt in a heavy pan and brown in the bacon drippings until onions are tender. Add canned tomatoes and then remaining ingredients. Simmer at least 1 hour. Additional water may be used to bring to the desired consistency. Chili is better if allowed to cool and then reheated prior to serving. Just before serving, add a can of chili beans, if desired.

When former President Lyndon B. Johnson traveled in Air Force One, the big jet's compartments were sure to hold a supply of what Mrs. Johnson called "Pedernales River chili." It was always frozen after it was cooked so all fat could be scraped off. Mrs. Johnson gave it a name when she had the recipe printed for mailing in response to requests. "It has been almost as popular as the government's pamphlet on the care and feeding of children," she says.

Mrs. Lyndon B. Johnson's Pedernales River Chili

4 pounds ground beef (chuck), coarsely ground
1 large onion, chopped
2 cloves garlic, minced
1 teaspoon ground oregano
1 teaspoon ground cumin

6 teaspoons chili powder (or more, to taste)
2 1-pound cans tomatoes, not drained
salt to taste
2 cups hot water

Put meat, onion, and garlic in large heavy pan and sear until light colored. Add oregano, cumin, chili powder, tomatoes, salt to taste, and hot water. Bring to boiling. Lower heat and simmer about 1 hour. As fat cooks out, skim. Makes 8–12 servings.

This one is mine:

Texas-OU Chili Pot

5 pounds stew meat, finely diced or coarsely ground
¼ cup hot oil
3 ounces or more Mexene chili powder
2 tablespoons salt
1 teaspoon garlic salt
1 teaspoon crushed oregano
3 teaspoons ground cumin
1 teaspoon onion powder
3 pints water
1 recipe pinto beans, drained, cooked with 2 tablespoons salt and 1 teaspoon black pepper. Reserve 1 cup for thickening chili.

Brown meat in hot oil until gray. Add seasoning and water and bring to a boil. Simmer on the lowest possible heat setting until really tender. Taste the meat and juice and correct seasoning, if necessary, to your liking. If you are cooking beans, too, mash one cupful and stir into chili for thickening. After beans are added to the chili, taste and adjust seasoning again.

The strong flavor of venison lends itself to chili. If you have some on hand, make this recipe from scratch, the way Mrs. Milton H. Thomas, Jr., a good, old-fashioned Dallas cook, does it.

Venison Chili

2 large onions, chopped
¼ cup salad oil
6 bay leaves
3 15½-ounce cans tomato sauce
4 teaspoons salt
4 pounds ground venison, hamburger grind
1 quart boiling water or chicken broth
1 teaspoon cayenne pepper
2 tablespoons chili powder
2 tablespoons ground cumin
2 cloves garlic

Sauté onions in salad oil until soft and yellow. Add bay leaves, tomato sauce, and salt. Simmer 1 minute. Crumble meat into this. Add water, cayenne pepper, chili powder, cumin, and garlic. Bring to a boil, reduce heat, and simmer 2 hours. Add more boiling water if too dry. Serves 8–10.

Seasoned hunters, such as Robert E. Peterson of Dallas, with an ongoing supply of venison often opt for having all but the backstrap ground fine for chili (saving the backstrap for chicken-fried steak), and frozen in 2-pound packages.

The Hunter's Choice

Peterson's wife Jane says, "Two pounds is right for two alarms of Wick Fowler's seasoning mix. I don't add suet, but I put a little bit of extra water to keep it from drying." Brown the venison. Add water according to package directions, but simmer 30 minutes to 1 hour, or until done, but no longer. The recipe serves 4, with some left over. The leftovers can be put into Parker House roll pockets, topped with grated cheese, and frozen to be served with tortilla soup at some later date.

5

Beans and Black-Eyes

Mike Flahive/TDA

Beans

An unusual set of historical and geographical circumstances, in addition to the combination of ethnic groups, has added some interesting facets to the style of Texas cuisine. Many dishes were created on the chuck wagon, and then flavored with a little Tex-Mex. As ranch-style cooking developed, recipes became defined into soups, stews, casseroles, meats, vegetables, and salads according to the amount of liquid, dressing, or condiments required to make them palatable.

As a result, a pot of beans may begin as a soup, peak as *frijoles refritos*, and tap out as an appetizer on a tortilla chip. Many a Texan's reputation for hospitality has its roots in the resourcefulness that grew with the land.

If variety is the spice of life, Texans have added more spark and beans to the melting pot than other Americans. Overlapping cultural frontiers along the Texas border allow us to draw from four other states, the Gulf, and Mexico, borrowing flavor from each. A final pinch of Texana adds special zest to the cuisine.

On one hand, in East Texas, where swamps and cypress knees look just like those in Louisiana, beans mixed with Texas long grain rice might remind you more of Cajuns than cowpokes. Nevertheless, the dish is popular all across Texas. On the other hand, chili powder added to hamhocks and lima beans gives a southwestern kick to the flavor of a southern casserole.

At the hand of a West Texas cowboy, simple pork and beans might rage hotter than a sudden prairie fire. In South Texas, however, refried Tex-Mex pintos might be the blandest selection on a plate of hot stuff. In any case, bean soup may be either the finished product or simply the first step.

Mike Flahive/TDA

Roundup cuisine: beans and stew plus biscuits, fruit cobbler, and a big pot of coffee

Generic Beans

Wash 1 pound of dried beans in cold water and pick through them for rocks and bad beans. If you think of it in time, soak the beans overnight; if not, plan for several hours of slow cooking. Beans need to cook forever, or until tender, whichever comes first. Place them in a large pot with a rinsed cube of salt pork or a ham bone, and cover with cold water, about 6 cups. Do not add salt until the last hour of cooking. To keep the right color and to prevent beans from breaking, stir occasionally with a wooden spoon. Heat to boiling and simmer for several hours until soft. Add water during cooking, if necessary, to keep beans from becoming dry. Season to taste, or according to the recipe in which they will be used.

According to cowpuncher and trail-ride cook Ramón Hartnett, the best thing to do with pinto beans is to cook them a second time, in a skillet. This deliberately bland dish combines well with stuffed jalapeño peppers or any *picante* Tex-Mex fare. Of course, those who really favor hot stuff will add chopped pepper to the recipe, as they do to everything.

Frijoles Refritos

1 cup shortening
6 cups cooked pinto beans
¼ cup grated cheese (optional)

Melt shortening in a large skillet over hot coals. Add pinto beans and mash. Heat through. Top with grated cheese, if desired.

Red Beans and Rice

2 cups red beans
2 cloves garlic
2 teaspoons seasoning salt
1 bay leaf
pinch of sugar
red pepper to taste
hamhock, if desired
1 large link smoked sausage, sliced
cooked long grain rice

Wash beans, soak overnight, and drain. Cover beans and all ingredients except sausage and rice with cold water. Bring to boil, reduce heat, and simmer until done. Remove garlic. Add smoked sausage during the last 30 minutes of cooking. At the same time, prepare rice according to box directions. Serve beans over individual bowls of rice. Serves 8.

For veteran trail-riding ranch cooks Richard Bolt and John White, this is the only serious pinto recipe:

Ranch Style Pinto Beans

1 pound pinto beans
¼ pound salt pork
1 onion
1-pound can tomatoes
3 tablespoons chili powder
1 teaspoon salt

Pick and wash beans, cover with water, and soak overnight. Add enough water to cover by 1 inch. Add salt pork and boil 30 minutes. Chop onion, add with remaining ingredients, and boil 2–3 hours longer, adding salt during the last hour and enough water to prevent sticking. Serves 8.

What Cajuns call New Orleans French Market 12-Bean Soup has been frankly usurped by many Texans, especially for a Christmas kitchen gift. Divided into proportional packages of pre-measured dry ingredients and presented with the recipe and a basket of optional extras, the soup makes a hearty New Year's greeting. Now that we've claimed this excellent soup for ourselves, let's remember a colorful Texan by calling it Judge Roy Bean Soup.

If you are a dyed-in-the-wool Texan, you already know about Roy Bean, self-appointed interpreter and enforcer of justice west of the Pecos. Well, certainly *someone* had to keep crime and fraud out of the little town of Langtry.

Judge Roy Bean Soup

Dried Bean Mix—
use equal amounts

lima beans
Great Northern beans
pinto beans
kidney beans
split peas
navy beans
black beans
red beans
garbanzos
barley
lentils
black-eyed peas

Use 2 cups dried bean mix to make 1 gallon of soup. Wash beans and cover with water. Soak overnight, or at least 3 hours. Drain, rinse, and place bean mixture in a big pot.

Add:

1 pound ham, diced
1 tablespoon salt
3–4 ribs celery, chopped
2 bay leaves
½ teaspoon thyme
water to cover, or 6 cups

Simmer 2½–3 hours, adding hot water as needed to keep beans covered. Then add:

2 1-pound cans undrained tomatoes
(1 Rotel, if you want spice)
2 medium onions, chopped
2 cloves garlic, pressed and minced
6 ribs celery, with leaves, chopped
¼ teaspoon red pepper, and salt and
pepper to taste
juice of 1 lemon, if desired

Cook 1½ hours to creamy stage. Meanwhile, prepare extra additions:

2 chicken breast quarters, or ½
chicken, skin removed
1 tablespoon salt
1 pound hot smoked sausage

Simmer chicken in water to cover with salt until chicken is tender. Remove chicken from bones and cut into small pieces. Parboil sausage separately, or sauté in skillet; remove and slice thin. Mix sausage and chicken into soup. Garnish with a handful of chopped, fresh parsley, if available, before serving. This soup freezes very well.

Black-Eyed Peas

The next time the subject of black-eyed peas comes up, notice the way a group polarizes into those who crave them and those who dismiss them altogether. The rift usually widens on New Year's Day when well-meaning black-eyed pea enthusiasts try to persuade the nonbelievers that they must eat at least *one* pea for good luck . . . but, for all their zeal, force-feeding wins few converts. All the believers can do is wait for misfortune to strike. Then, at least, they can declare a triumphant "I told you so!"

Mike Flahive/TDA

Black-eyed peas call for green onions, tomatoes, and cornbread sticks on the side.

In July 1980, Bob Gates researched historical phenomena to determine why anyone would disapprove of the black-eyed pea.

"Why?" he asked. "Could it be because of its family?" Bob traced the black-eye or cowpea from livestock feed back to its ancient recorded history in early Sanskrit writings. From India, he chased it into the Middle East and Africa, through fourteenth-century Europe, and into the holds of slave ships. He pinned it down on the American side of the Atlantic in the 1791 writing of George Washington, who bought 40 bushels of seed for his plantation. Then, in a fast-forward mode, Gates focused on the wit of Austin broadcast personality Cactus Pryor:

"A plan is afoot to deprive Americans of that most delicious of all foodstuff . . . the fresh black-eyed pea. Knowing full well that some of us . . . regard this little delicacy as the pearl of vegetables, the plotters assume that by making this treasure unavailable it will cause widespread friction and confusion and even hysteria."

Perhaps fresh black-eyes are hard to find because those who care enough to grow them keep the fruits of their labor to themselves. If you find them fresh, Austin's Fran Gerling, who has developed many recipes for the Texas Department of Agriculture, recommends the following tender, loving recipe.

Fran's Fresh Black-Eyed Peas

2 cups black-eyed peas and snaps
2½ cups water
½ teaspoon salt or more to taste
⅛ teaspoon white pepper
¼ teaspoon black pepper, freshly ground
¼ cup onion, minced
1 clove garlic, minced
⅛ teaspoon ground thyme
3 sprigs fresh basil, minced, if available
6 slices bacon, fried, drained, and diced

Pour all ingredients in 3-quart saucepan. Bring contents to a boil. Immediately reduce heat to simmer for 30–40 minutes or until peas are tender. Taste to adjust seasonings and add more salt or pepper to your own taste. Serves 6–8.

Note: You may substitute frozen black-eyed peas for the fresh, but they usually do not need to be cooked quite so long to be tender, since they are already blanched.

For a typical country Texas meal served around the Fourth of July, try black-eyed peas, cornbread, sliced tomatoes, and green onions.

The dried black-eyed beauties, as well as canned, are better suited to some dishes. Try Fran's marinated salad with those, too. Then, you might experiment with some of the prize winners Bob Gates reported from Athens, the Black-Eyed Pea Capital of the World, on the occasion of the Tenth Annual Black-Eyed Pea Jamboree in July 1980.

From William C. Johnston, of Huntsville:

Henderson County Quiche

2–3 cups cooked dried black-eyed peas, drained and mashed
1 teaspoon garlic powder
½ cup finely chopped or grated onion
1 cup cooked ham, chopped fine
1 tablespoon chopped parsley
¼ cup chopped pepper (hot or sweet)
about ¾ cup cooked fresh black-eyed peas
1 cup shredded cheese
6 eggs, well beaten
1 cup evaporated milk
½ cup black-eyed pea juice
¼ teaspoon black pepper
1½ teaspoons pork sausage seasoning

Mix mashed peas with garlic powder and form into a pastry shell in a buttered 10-inch pie plate. Cook in 350° F. oven for 10 minutes. Remove and place onion, ham, parsley, pepper, peas, and cheese in shell. Combine eggs, milk,

pea juice, pepper, and sausage seasoning, and mix thoroughly. Pour into shell over other ingredients. Cook in 350° F. oven about 30 minutes or until knife inserted in center comes out clean. Makes 8 slices.

If you happen to have 4 cups of black-eyes already cooked, try another recipe from Fran Gerling:

Marinated Black-Eyed Pea Salad

4 cups black-eyed peas, cooked
1 cup celery, finely sliced
4 ounces green chiles, chopped
¼ cup red bell pepper, finely diced
½ cup purple onion, diced
2 cloves garlic, finely minced
1 teaspoon salt or more to taste
½ teaspoon black pepper
1 teaspoon Worcestershire sauce
1½ cups Italian dressing or enough to cover peas
garnish: red cabbage leaves and minced green onion tops

In a large glass bowl, combine all ingredients except garnish, stirring to mix well. If the liquid does not cover the peas in your bowl, add a little more dressing. Marinate, covered, for 24 hours in refrigerator. Drain excess salad dressing and spoon salad onto a shallow salad bowl lined with red cabbage leaves. Sprinkle with green onion tops. This salad refrigerates well for a week. Serves 8–10.

From James Stacks, of Athens:

Mini Chalu-peas

3-pound pork roast
4 cups water
½ cup chopped onion
2 cloves garlic, chopped
1 tablespoon salt
2 tablespoons chili powder
1 tablespoon cumin
1 teaspoon oregano
4-ounce can chopped green chiles
2-ounce jar pimientos
4 cups black-eyed peas, cooked

Bring all ingredients except peas to a boil in a heavy 6-quart pan or slow cooker, and simmer over low heat for 5 hours. Remove roast and break into small pieces. Return to heat and cook another 1–2 hours. Drain off any remaining broth, add peas, and mash all together. Serve on tortilla chips. Garnish with lettuce, tomatoes, cheese, jalapeño peppers, or guacamole salad. Serves a crowd as appetizers.

From Linda Martin, of Athens:

Peas and Ham Hot

3½ cups cooked ham, cut in cubes
1½ cups cut celery
½ cup diced green pepper
1 medium onion, chopped
8-ounce can water chestnuts, sliced
3½ cups cooked black-eyed peas,
   drained
1¼ cups mayonnaise
1½ teaspoons lemon juice
⅓ cup crushed potato chips
8 cupped lettuce leaves

Combine first eight ingredients and mix lightly. Pour into a greased 2-quart baking dish. Top with crushed potato chips. Bake in a 350° F. oven for 25 minutes. Serve hot in lettuce cups. Serves 8.

And from Connie Fay Johnson, of Athens:

Dilly Peas

immature pea pods (approx. 200)
6 cloves garlic
3 pods hot pepper
3 teaspoons dill weed
2½ cups vinegar
2½ cups water
⅓ cup salt

Trim ends off pea pods and wash. Pack into three sterilized pint jars with 2 cloves of garlic, 1 pod of pepper, and 1 teaspoon of dill weed in each jar. Heat vinegar, water, and salt to rolling boil. Fill each jar and seal. Place jars on a rack in a large pan or kettle. Fill with boiling water until jars are covered by 1–2 inches of water. Cover, adjust heat to maintain a gentle boil, and boil 10 minutes. Remove from water. Let sit for 2 weeks. Chill before serving.

54

John Suhrstedt

6

Salads, Veggies, and Rice

Dan Morrison/TDA

Salads

One of the best salads in Dallas, as served at the Mansion on Turtle Creek, suits those who like a light but tasty lunch. If you don't have cooked beef tongue (and can't buy it), substitute cold strips of another kind . . . unless you have four hours to cook a tongue.

Rice Council of America

Paella Salad combines rice with shellfish and chicken.

Mansion Sunset Salad
(individual, luncheon size)

4 ounces romaine lettuce, chopped
    coarsely
4 ounces white cabbage, sliced
    medium
2 green bell pepper slices, ¼-inch
    round
2 ounces cooked chicken breast, cut 2
    inches long and ½ inch wide
2 ounces cooked beef tongue strips,
    cut 2 inches long and ½ inch wide
2 ounces cured ham, cut 2 inches by
    1½ inches
1 hard-boiled egg, peeled and
    quartered
½ small tomato, sliced and shaped
    into a rose garnish

Wash romaine and cabbage in cool water. Drain well and set aside. Slice green pepper, chicken, beef tongue, and ham. Arrange lettuce and cabbage side by side in a wooden bowl. Arrange meats on top of the greens. Place two green pepper slices on top of the meats. Place the quartered boiled eggs around the lettuce.

To prepare tomato garnish: Place ½ small tomato open side down. With a sharp knife, slice vertically, keeping the tomato together. Wrap slices around one another to make a rose garnish. Serve with a choice of salad dressing.

———

TexaSweet, the association of citrus growers in the Rio Grande Valley, shared this unusual salad recipe with *Texas Highways* readers.

Holiday Turkey Salad

2 cups cubed cooked turkey
1 cup sliced celery
½ cup mayonnaise, thinned with
    orange juice
¼ cup slivered almonds, toasted
lettuce
1 cup fresh orange segments

Combine turkey, celery, mayonnaise, and almonds. Chill. Serve on lettuce. Garnish with orange segments.

Note: Tuna or chicken can be used in place of the turkey.

When you crave a Greek salad to go with your *souflaki*, here's the one from the U.T. Institute of Texan Cultures, as prepared by Mrs. Katherine Green of San Antonio:

Greek Salad or Salata

1 clove garlic, cut in half
1 head lettuce, torn into bite-sized
    pieces
½ cup chopped celery
3 tomatoes, cut into wedges
1 small scallion, chopped fine
½ green pepper, sliced
5 radishes, sliced
salt and pepper to taste
1 teaspoon oregano
¼ cup olive oil
2 tablespoons wine vinegar

    Garnish
calamata olives
anchovies
¼ cup crumbled feta cheese

Rub wooden salad bowl with garlic. Wash vegetables and mix them in the bowl. Mix seasonings together with the oil and vinegar. Add to the vegetables and toss. Garnish with calamata olives, anchovies, and feta cheese. Makes 4–6 servings.

Grapefruit Spinach Salad

10-ounce package fresh spinach
2 Ruby Red grapefruit, peeled and
    sectioned
sesame dressing (recipe follows)

Wash, dry, and chill spinach leaves. Section grapefruit, removing membrane. At serving time, mix fruit and spinach and add dressing to taste.

Sesame Dressing

¼ cup lemon juice
3 tablespoons white wine vinegar
2 tablespoons sugar
1 teaspoon dry mustard
½ teaspoon salt
dash onion powder
1 cup salad oil
3 tablespoons sesame seeds

Mix thoroughly first six ingredients. Slowly whisk in salad oil, beating well. Stir in seeds. Makes 1⅓ cups.

Pascal Gode and Pascal Vignau, co-chefs of the French Room of the Adolphus Hotel, gave me this salad, which is their idea of *le piquenique:*

Rice Salad with Salmon

2½ cups cooked rice, rinsed and
    cooled
1 pound fresh salmon, poached in
    court bouillon (see below) and
    cooled
1 bunch celery, trimmed and thinly
    sliced
2 finely diced bell peppers (1 red,
    1 green, if possible)
1 medium onion, chopped fine
4 tomatoes (1 sliced, 3 diced)
4 hard-boiled eggs
8 1-inch sections of green onions
    (green part only)

    Dressing
2 egg yolks
3 tablespoons Dijon mustard
2 tablespoons red wine vinegar
2 cups salad oil
2 tablespoons fresh tarragon, chopped
4 tablespoons fresh parsley, chopped

    Court Bouillon
boiling salted water
1 sliced onion
6 peppercorns
1 sliced carrot
1 branch celery
1 bay leaf
2 tablespoons lemon juice

Prepare rice and set aside. Poach salmon for 7 minutes in boiling court bouillon over low heat. Remove salmon and cool. Clean, slice, and chop celery, bell peppers, onion, and 3 tomatoes and mix with the rice. To make the dressing, beat egg yolks with mustard; add wine vinegar, then a thin stream of salad oil. Mix in tarragon and parsley. Add dressing and segments of salmon to rice mixture. Decorate with quartered hard-boiled eggs, green onions, and slices of tomato. Chill for at least 1 hour before serving. Serves 5 or 6.

And speaking of rice salads, here's another, from *Texas Highways*.

Paella Salad

1 cup yellow rice (see below)
6-ounce package frozen cooked, peeled, and deveined shrimp
8-ounce can minced clams, drained
1½ cups diced cooked chicken
1½ cups sliced celery
1½ cups cooked green peas
½ cup diced green pepper
⅓ cup sliced green onions with tops
1 cup mayonnaise
2 tablespoons dry white wine
3 tablespoons capers (optional)
½ teaspoon salt
¼ teaspoon garlic powder
¼ teaspoon ground black pepper
2 medium fresh tomatoes, cut in wedges

Cook rice in chicken broth according to package directions with a pinch of saffron, turmeric, or paprika.

Thaw shrimp and slice in half, lengthwise. Combine with rice, clams, chicken, celery, green peas, green pepper, and onions. Blend in mayonnaise with remaining ingredients except tomatoes. Pour over shrimp mixture and toss lightly. Chill. Use tomatoes for garnish, or toss with salad before chilling. Makes 8½ cups or 6–8 servings.

The following salad is from Mrs. Alice Lehne Fogg, of San Antonio.

Sauerkraut Salad

1 large onion, diced
1 bell pepper, diced
1 cup celery, diced
4-ounce jar pimientos, diced
1 large unpeeled apple, diced
2 cups sauerkraut, drained
1 cup sugar
¾ teaspoon salt
½ cup wine vinegar
¼ cup vegetable oil

Mix all ingredients well and refrigerate 24 hours before serving. Makes about 12 servings.

According to statistics gathered by the U.T. Institute of Texan Cultures, Texans of German descent comprise the Lone Star State's fourth-largest ethnic group. German immigration dates back to Friedrich Ernst, who came to Stephen F. Austin's colony in the Mexican Texas of 1831. Since that time, Texans have adopted many of the dishes and traditions of German origin.

In 1983, *Texas Highways* visited the Slaton Wurstfest, which has grown from an amateur parish benefit in 1971 to a four-day event requiring the grinding and smoking of thousands of pounds of sausage.

An even bigger event, the Wurstfest at New Braunfels, was established in 1961 to celebrate German food and tradition brought to the Hill Country by settlers in the 1840s. Today, the ten-day event draws more than 150,000 people.

If you've never been to a wurstfest, try to go to one or the other. At either event, the fare will be German in origin: wurst, sauerkraut, beans, potato salad, homemade breads and cakes. Get in the mood for wurstfest anytime . . . buy the sausage from your favorite German producer, and make this potato salad to go with it (from Phoebe Schumacher, of Monthalia, as published in *The Melting Pot*).

German Potato Salad

6 medium potatoes
salt
1 onion, diced
3 tablespoons white vinegar
¼ teaspoon pepper
1 teaspoon celery seed
½ pound bacon, diced
2 teaspoons sugar

Boil potatoes in salted water until tender. Peel and cube while still warm. Add diced onion, vinegar, pepper, and celery seed. Fry diced bacon until crisp and drain off all but ½ cup of the drippings. Sprinkle sugar over the bacon and remaining drippings. Mix well and pour over the potatoes and onions. Serve immediately.

People who take their barbecue seriously have a favorite way to make potato salad. My recipe is for those who don't like it sweet, yellow, or mashed.

Potato Salad

4 extra large eggs, hard-boiled
6 large potatoes, peeled and cut in large dice, then boiled in salted water
2 tablespoons white vinegar
1 tablespoon dried parsley
2 teaspoons salt
1 teaspoon black pepper
½ teaspoon onion salt
½ teaspoon celery salt
¼ teaspoon celery seed (optional)
¼ teaspoon dry mustard
½ cup chopped "hamburger dill" sliced pickles
¾ cup mayonnaise
olives and paprika

Boil and peel eggs; refrigerate to firm them for cutting. Boil potatoes 20–25 minutes, or until a fork pierces the pieces, but does not shatter them. Drain in colander and place in mixing bowl.

Sprinkle potatoes while still warm with white vinegar, parsley, salt, pepper, onion salt, celery salt and seed, and dry mustard. Turn gently with a wooden spoon to distribute, being careful not to mash the potato cubes. Cool.

Fold in chopped pickles, mayonnaise, and the eggs, sliced and chopped, at the last. Cover and keep refrigerated. Before serving, place on lettuce leaves and sprinkle top with paprika. May be decorated with sliced, stuffed olives, if desired, or whole pitted black olives.

Note: Seasoning may need a slight adjustment, depending on size of potatoes. Serves 8.

L'Entrecote restaurant, in Loews Anatole Hotel at the Dallas Market Center, boasts a young Alsatian chef de cuisine, Michel Bernard Platz, master of the French Moderne (and inventor of the pickled red rose).

"I used to put flowers beside every plate," he says, "but, now, I put edible flowers *on* each plate; they don't improve the flavor of anything, but they are beautiful garnishes. The flowers come from Hawaii, except for the mustard flowers from Texas." *Everything on a plate must be edible,* Michel says, with emphasis, so *be sure to use the right flowers.* He doesn't have to elaborate on the possible consequences.

Michel makes an unusual, colorful salad, even without flowers. If you have the flowers on your farm or in your garden, use them. Otherwise, leave them off. Make the dressing below at least one night before serving. You'll have some left over to keep in the refrigerator.

Warm Golden Apple Salad with Pink Radishes

4 golden apples
salt and ground white pepper
¼ cup + 1 tablespoon butter
2 cups radishes, cut in julienne strips
4 fresh basil leaves (opal basil, if possible), chopped
dash of black currant vinegar
6 ounces basil vinaigrette (recipe follows)
garnish of fresh mustard flowers and *edible* leaves, such as chervil, chives, cress, or mint, and basil

Pare and core apples and slice each into 8 wedges. Sprinkle lightly with salt and pepper and sauté both sides in ¼ cup butter until golden. Transfer to a 350° F. oven to finish while preparing the radishes.

Cut radishes in fine julienne strips, season with salt and pepper, and add chopped basil leaves. Sauté quickly in 1 tablespoon butter. Deglaze pan with a dash of black currant vinegar. It will add a pink color to the radishes.

Place apple slices in a star pattern on each salad plate, with radishes in the center. Pour 1½ ounces basil dressing over each. Garnish with chopped chives or fresh chervil leaves around, a fresh basil leaf on top, and the fresh Texas mustard flower on top. Serve while warm. Makes 4 servings.

New luxury hotels worth their salt-substitute now offer facilities for fitness and recreation, along with at least a few low-calorie dishes on the menu. The Mandalay Four Seasons Hotel at Las Colinas in Irving, Texas, goes an extra step. A health-oriented restaurant called Alternatives offers a menu geared to the diet-dedicated patrons of the Four Seasons Fitness Resort and Spa. The salad recipe below is representative of the health fare presented by Spa Chef Christiane Chavanne.

Raiz Salad

1 pound jicama
2 medium carrots, peeled
3 Jerusalem artichokes (raw), peeled
1 peeled turnip
8 red radishes, sliced
4 red cabbage leaves
16 endive spears
16 strips red bell pepper
3 scallions, finely chopped
2 tablespoons pumpkin seeds, shelled
1 tablespoon sunflower seeds, shelled (unsalted)
1 small beet, blanched, peeled, and diced
8 tiny ears baby corn, preferably fresh

Cut jicama, carrots, Jerusalem artichokes, and turnip into Julienne strips. Toss with sliced radishes. Arrange individual servings on cabbage leaves, each surrounded by endive spears. Garnish endive spears with strips of red pepper. Mound mixture onto cabbage leaves and top each serving with scallions, pumpkin and sunflower seeds, and diced beet. Garnish each serving with two ears of corn and, if desired, extra strips of bell pepper. Serve with Valley Citrus Dressing, below. Serves 4.

Valley Citrus Dressing

1 cup water
1 tablespoon arrowroot, dissolved in 1 tablespoon cold water
combined juices of 2 tangerines, 2 grapefruit, 2 oranges, 2 limes, and 2 lemons
1 shallot, minced
2 garlic cloves, minced
1 tablespoon vegetable and herb flakes, such as Vegit or Spike (available in seasoning and health sections of supermarket)
1 pinch powdered cumin
1 pinch cayenne pepper
1 tablespoon coriander powder

Note: 1 pinch = less than ⅛ teaspoon

Bring water just to a boil. Stir in dissolved arrowroot and cook, stirring constantly, 1 minute or until glossy. Cool mixture. Add juices and spices and chill. Serve with the salad.

Basil Vinaigrette

2 tablespoons shallots, finely chopped
2 tablespoons fresh (opal) basil, chopped
1 cup walnut oil
1 cup vegetable salad oil
¾ cup white wine vinegar (or basil vinegar)
1 tablespoon mustard
salt and freshly ground pepper to taste

Mix all ingredients together and allow to rest overnight. Check seasoning before serving.

———————————

Whenever *Texas Highways'* Tommie Pinkard finds herself on the road around Stonewall, Texas, she stops at the fresh produce co-op at Burg's Corner. One stop inspired Tommie's

Non-Waldorf Salad

1 small head red cabbage
2 tart, crisp Texas apples
2 tablespoons lemon juice
1 tablespoon sugar, if desired
1 cup Texas pecans, coarsely chopped
¾ cup mayonnaise or cole slaw dressing, or a mixture of the two

Slice or shred cabbage into thin strips. Dice apples (unpared) and sprinkle with lemon juice and sugar. Toss cabbage, apples, and pecans with dressing. Cover and chill. Serves 6.

Vegetables

Among the recipes from the Good Old Days, collected by Imperial Sugar, some vegetable dishes seem deliberately loaded with extra calories to refuel hard-working farmers at noon. Others, such as the Cabbage Gumbo recipe, seem to be designed to use a lot of produce from the farm garden. "Or the freezer case," suggests Imperial spokesperson June Towers.

TDA

Cabbage Gumbo

2 tablespoons lard (or shortening)
1 large onion, chopped
2 green peppers, chopped
1 small head of cabbage, chopped
3 tomatoes, peeled and chopped
1 cup sliced okra
2 tablespoons vinegar
1 tablespoon granulated sugar
salt to taste

Melt lard (shortening), and cook onion and peppers slowly over low heat for a few minutes. Then add the chopped cabbage, tomatoes, okra, vinegar, and sugar. Add salt to taste. Add enough water to barely cover and cook about 30 minutes. Serves 6–8.

Poke Salat

Say you don't know what *poke salat* is? Well, *Webster's New World Dictionary* doesn't either. "Puccoon or Pocan—a weed used for staining," it says. Furthermore, Pokeweed, or *Phytolacca americana*, has poisonous roots, stems, and berries. That's the bad news; the good news is that the leaves are edible.

Texas Highways found someone who not only knows what poke salat is, but also knows how to make it. Howard Peacock knows: "'Pigeonberry' is another common monicker for this free-for-the-taking comestible, packed with iron and other nutrients famed for scouring the blood." If you don't know poke when you see it, don't pick it. Buy collard greens from your grocer instead.

This recipe, to be used only with the leaves from young sprouts, not older plants, comes from Mrs. Bergen Dean of Tyler County, as reported by Peacock in March 1982: "Mrs. Dean washes the trimmed leaves at a faucet under a huge oak. Then, at her stove, she parboils the leaves for about a minute. Most cooks pour off one or two waters from a mess of poke to make sure an irritant in the skin of older plants is removed.

"A piece of fatback pork, ½ teaspoon of salt, one teaspoon sugar, and a dab of bacon grease flavor Mrs. Dean's greens. They cook on low heat for about 30 minutes."

Trust the U. T. Institute of Texan Cultures to bring you the only way collard greens should be cooked:

Collard Greens

2 bunches of greens
¼ pound bacon or hog jowl
2 tablespoons bacon drippings
1 red pepper pod (optional)

Pick and wash greens. Cut bacon into pieces and fry in drippings, but do not brown. Boil greens for 30 minutes. Shred and wash greens again. Add bacon and pepper pod, cover, and boil 30 minutes or until tender. Serve with hot cornbread. Serves 6.

Another vegetable with a long history:

Corn Fritters

2 cups canned whole-kernel corn, drained
1 teaspoon salt
1 tablespoon granulated sugar
2 eggs
1 cup flour, or enough to make a stiff batter
1 tablespoon baking powder
shortening for frying

Combine the canned corn (our grandmothers canned corn from their gardens) with the remaining ingredients. If batter becomes too stiff, soften with ¼ cup milk. Drop by spoonfuls into hot shortening. Fry until deep golden brown on all sides. About 6 servings.

Daphne Derven's adaptation of old-fashioned hominy pudding combines the best of several old recipes.

Hominy Pudding

2 cups hominy
¼ pound butter
½ cup heavy cream
¼ cup brown (or granulated) sugar
½ teaspoon ground mace
½ teaspoon grated nutmeg
½ teaspoon lemon cordial
6 egg whites, stiffly beaten

Mix together all ingredients, folding in egg whites at the last. Bake in a buttered casserole at 325° F. for 30 minutes. Serves 6.

This recipe is from Austin's Green Pastures Restaurant:

Christmas Hominy Casserole

2 cups canned yellow hominy, drained and rinsed in cold water
1 cup canned cream of mushroom soup
1 teaspoon Worcestershire sauce
½ teaspoon salt
cornflakes rolled into crumbs
1 tablespoon butter
½ pound fresh mushrooms, sliced and sautéed in butter (optional)
3 tablespoons heavy cream (optional)

Mix hominy, mushroom soup, Worcestershire sauce, and salt. Pour into a buttered casserole, sprinkle with the crushed cornflakes, and dot with butter. Bake at 300° F. until brown. Serves 6.

For a richer casserole, add fresh mushrooms and heavy cream to the mixture before pouring it into the casserole.

Among the recipes collected by members of the Jane Douglas Chapter of the Daughters of the American Revolution for Imperial Sugar, *Texas Highways* chose this one:

Candied Sweet Potatoes

6 sweet potatoes
1¼ cups brown sugar
¼ teaspoon salt
1 tablespoon lemon juice
1 tablespoon butter

Pare sweet potatoes and parboil them 15 minutes. Cut them in thick lengthwise slices. Place them in a casserole with the remaining ingredients between the layers. Pour about ¾ cup water over the sweet potatoes, and bake in a 350° F. oven 35 minutes, covered. Remove cover; bake 10 minutes to brown. Serves 6 very hungry field hands or 8–10 city folks.

From the National Pecan Marketing Council, Bryan:

Broccoli and Pecans

4 large stalks broccoli
1 tablespoon butter
¼ cup broken pecans
1 tablespoon lemon juice

Trim broccoli of leaves and pithy stem ends. Cut lengthwise into quarters and arrange in a large skillet. Add 1 inch of water; cover and cook until tender, about 15 minutes. Melt butter in a small skillet; add pecans and heat through. Stir in lemon juice. Drain broccoli, pour butter sauce over it, and serve.

———————————————

In December 1983, Austin's Mary Faulk Koock shared some Christmas feasting traditions from her family home, which she transformed into the Green Pastures Restaurant. She began with a good smoked ham finished with a simple glaze, and homemade relishes like watermelon-rind pickles and a cranberry sauce.

Sweet Potatoes (Koocked) in Orange Cups

10 East Texas sweet potatoes
1 stick (¼ pound) unsalted butter
2 tablespoons brown sugar
½ teaspoon salt
¼ cup bourbon
½ cup chopped pecans
½ teaspoon cinnamon
¼ teaspoon nutmeg
6 oranges
chopped pecans or marshmallows for garnish

Boil potatoes in jackets until tender. Peel, mash well, or push through a vegetable press; add butter while potatoes are hot, and then add remaining ingredients (except oranges). Taste and correct seasoning if necessary. Cut oranges in half, scalloping the edges with a sharp paring knife. Remove pulp from the oranges, and squeeze to make ¼ cup juice; add this to potato mixture (or substitute 2 tablespoons grated orange peel).

Fill orange shells with potato mixture, and cover with foil. Bake at 325° F. about 30 minutes. Remove foil, and garnish with chopped pecans or marshmallows. Return to oven for a few minutes, and then serve hot. Serves 12.

———————————————

A chuck wagon cook named John White earned a reputation for producing a hearty menu for the working cowboys on the J. A. Matthews Ranch at Albany. He had a way of making sliced vegetables into substantial fare.

Fried Tomatoes or Squash

Peel and slice 4 large, semi-green tomatoes. Dip in a mixture of flour and cornmeal and fry in 1 inch of hot shortening until brown. Salt to taste.

Fry summer squash the same way. Slice 6 medium yellow squash; wash and dip in a mixture of flour and cornmeal. Fry in deep fat until brown. Salt to taste.

A combination of the two vegetables livens up a drab plate of plain meat and potatoes.

Crab Stuffed Potatoes

1 pound flaked crabmeat
6 large baking potatoes
½ cup softened margarine
¼ cup milk, or more as needed
½ teaspoon salt
¼ teaspoon black pepper
¼ teaspoon paprika
sprigs of parsley
lemon wedges

Remove all remaining shell and cartilage from crabmeat. Refrigerate meat until ready to use. Bake potatoes in oven at 400° F. for 45 minutes or in microwave oven according to instructions. Carefully scoop out potato, saving shells. Mash potato; beat in margarine, milk as needed, salt, and pepper. Mix in crabmeat. Pile mixture in potato shells. Sprinkle with paprika. Reheat in oven, allowing mixture to brown slightly. Garnish with parsley and lemon wedges. Serves 6.

Daphne Derven adapted century-old recipes and developed her own for sweet potatoes:

Sweet Potato Pudding

Peel and cut up 2 pounds of sweet potatoes, and cook in a little water until tender. Crush and mix with 8 ounces of butter, 6 ounces of sugar, a nutmeg grated, a teaspoonful of grated cinnamon, a half teaspoonful of powdered mace, juice and grated peel of a lemon, 8 beaten eggs, and 2 ounces each of brandy and roseflower water. Stir thoroughly and bake for 45 minutes at 350° F. Serves 8.

———————————————

Another, from Lyndon B. Johnson's former cook:

Mrs. Fantroy's East Texas Candied Yams

2 pounds sweet potatoes
1 teaspoon lemon juice
1 teaspoon salt
½ stick (4 tablespoons) margarine, melted
1 cup sugar
½ cup light brown sugar
¼ cup corn syrup
¼ teaspoon nutmeg

Peel yams and cut in quarters. Boil in water to cover and lemon juice 20–30 minutes until tender. Pour water off; put yams in 2-quart baking dish and cover with other ingredients that have been mixed together. Bake uncovered at 350° F. for 30 minutes or until done. Serves 8.

———————————————

Another recipe from Daphne Derven's re-creation of an 1850s-style Christmas dinner:

Winter Squash

Winter squash, or cushaw, is fit to eat by August, and in a dry warm place it can be kept well all winter. The color is a bright yellow. Pare it, take out the seeds, cut it in pieces, and stew slowly in a very little water till quite soft. Drain, squeeze, and press it well, and mash it with a very little butter, salt, and curry powder.

J. Griffis Smith

A split-rail fence and maple trees on a farm near Mineola recall New England scenes.

For a brief time, Dallasites enjoyed the Old House on Mockingbird, just off the long strip of here-today restaurants on Greenville Avenue. As a house, it was something to see! Built in 1914 by pioneering electronic whiz John Oram, on solid concrete and steel beams, the then country home featured an observation deck for the astronomical instruments Oram treasured. They were mementos of the study of an 1880 eclipse of the sun, when Oram assisted Thomas Edison in the first synchronization of time throughout the United States.

Unfortunately, all that is left of the Old House is the recipe for fried zucchini, reported in *Texas Highways*.

Fried Zucchini

1 pound fresh zucchini
6 ounces milk
4 tablespoons flour
8 tablespoons cracker meal
1 tablespoon Parmesan cheese
deep fat for frying

Trim ends from zucchini; slice diagonally in ¼-inch slices. Soak slices 20 minutes in milk. Drain and coat with flour. Dip in milk again, then coat in a mixture of cracker meal and Parmesan cheese. Fry in deep fat until golden brown. Drain, and serve with tartar sauce. Serves 4.

Try this sauce with plain cooked vegetables:

Sauce for Vegetables

½ cup butter
1 tablespoon fresh lemon juice
1 tablespoon chopped parsley
⅓ cup fresh bread crumbs, toasted
1 cup Texas peanuts, coarsely chopped

Melt butter; stir in lemon juice and parsley. Add bread crumbs and peanuts. Heat and pour over your favorite cooked vegetables.

From Fredericksburg's Oma Koock Restaurant:

Oma's Sauerkraut

3 strips bacon, minced and medium-cooked (reserve grease)
1 green apple
1 medium onion
16-ounce can sauerkraut
salt and pepper
½ cup sherry
1 tablespoon chopped parsley

Peel and thin-slice apple and onion. Sauté in bacon grease. Add sauerkraut, salt and pepper to taste, sherry, and bacon. Cover and place in a 350° F. oven for 30 minutes. Arrange on platter; top with chopped parsley.

Rice

For some reason, the importance of the rice crop in Texas has been grossly understated. Marty Hidalgo looked into the matter for *Texas Highways* (September 1982) and learned that more progress had been made in Texas in the cultivation and marketing of rice since 1940 than anywhere else in all years since 3000 B.C.

"Most Texans can't say 'rice' in German, Arabic, Afrikaans, Greek, or Dutch," wrote Marty, "but Texas marketers can say it in those languages because those countries and others have developed a preference for our long grains. Stevedores heave tons of the crop into the bellies of ships at Galveston and Houston to keep pace with the demand."

Rice Council of America

At the turn of the century, Jefferson County in East Texas possessed the state's only rice mill, irrigation canals, and rice crop. Today, Texas is the third largest producing state with more than 580,000 acres planted in rice, and is the nation's number one rice milling center.

Rice Chantilly

3 cups cooked rice
½ cup sour cream
1 teaspoon salt
1 or 2 dashes ground red pepper
1 cup (4 ounces) grated Cheddar
  cheese, divided

Combine rice, sour cream, salt, pepper, and ½ cup cheese. Spoon into a buttered shallow 1-quart baking dish. Top with remaining cheese. Bake at 350° F. 20 minutes. Makes 4–6 servings.

Years before my mother learned to cook, her mother and grandmother served this rice and vermicelli dish with any Middle Eastern fare cooked in a spicy tomato sauce. Browning the vermicelli in butter gives it a color and flavor lacking in the commercially packaged mixture.

Rice with Vermicelli

1 cup long grain rice, uncooked
¼ cup butter or margarine
½ cup vermicelli, broken into 1-inch
  pieces
1 tablespoon salt
1½ cups hot water

Place rice in a colander and rinse under tap water. Drain and set aside. Melt butter in heavy saucepan on lowest heat setting. Add vermicelli and brown, stirring constantly to prevent burning. Add drained rice and salt to saucepan, stirring until rice absorbs butter. Add 1½ cups hot water and stir once. Bring water to a boil, lower heat, and cover saucepan. Cook for 20 minutes, or until rice is tender and water has been absorbed. Serves 4–6.

Strictly speaking, Harvest Rice can't be called a casserole, but it serves the same purpose:

Harvest Rice

1 cup thinly sliced carrots
2 tablespoons butter or margarine
1¼ cups water
¾ cup apple juice
2 tablespoons lemon juice
2 tablespoons brown sugar
1 teaspoon salt
1 cup uncooked rice
½ teaspoon ground cinnamon
¼ cup raisins
½ cup sliced green onions, with tops
2 apples, cored and sliced in thin
  wedges (do not peel)
1 tablespoon sesame seed, toasted

In a large skillet or saucepan, cook carrots in butter until tender crisp, about 3 minutes. Add liquids, brown sugar, and salt. Bring to a boil. Stir in rice, cinnamon, and raisins. Reduce heat, cover, and simmer until rice is tender and liquid is absorbed, about 15 minutes. Gently stir in green onions and apples; heat thoroughly. Turn into serving dish. Top with sesame seed. Makes 6 servings.

The Rice Council offers this idea for a classy casserole for two.

Rice Casserole

1 cup cooked rice
6½-ounce can flaked crabmeat,
  drained
⅓ cup diced carrot
¼ cup (1 ounce) grated Cheddar
  cheese
¼ cup sliced green onions, including
  tops
¼ cup sour cream
½ teaspoon salt
⅛ teaspoon ground black pepper
paprika

Preheat oven to 350° F. Combine all ingredients except paprika. Turn into 1-quart baking dish or 2 individual baking dishes. Dust with paprika. Cover and bake for 20–25 minutes, or until hot. Serves 2.

Sodium watchers will welcome this entry from the Rice Council. Each serving of Rice and Shrimp Supreme contains 160 milligrams of sodium.

Rice and Shrimp Supreme

1 tablespoon unsalted butter or
  margarine
2 tablespoons flour
1½ cups half-and-half (milk/cream)
½ teaspoon dill weed
½ teaspoon paprika
⅛ teaspoon hot pepper sauce
1 pound peeled deveined raw shrimp
½ cup sliced green onions, including
  tops
¼ cup diced pimientos
3 tablespoons grated Parmesan cheese
3 cups hot cooked rice

Melt butter in 3-quart saucepan. Stir in flour. Add half-and-half, dill, paprika, and pepper sauce. Cook, stirring constantly, over medium heat until thickened and bubbly. Add shrimp; cook until shrimp turns pink (3–5 minutes). Stir in onions, pimientos, and cheese. Heat through and serve over bed of fluffy rice. Serves 6.

Oyster Rice Dressing

(Enough to fill one hen or to make one
  casserole)

¼ cup butter
6–8 green onions, chopped, using
  both white and green parts
½ cup chopped celery
¼ cup chopped bell pepper
1 pint oysters, including liquor
½ pound hen giblets, cooked and
  chopped
2 cups cooked rice
salt, red and black pepper to taste

Melt butter in heavy skillet. Sauté onions, celery, and bell pepper slowly until soft. Add oysters and giblets. Pour over rice. Mix and add salt and peppers to taste. If too dry, add some of the liquid in which the giblets cooked. Stuff hen and bake at 350° F. for 2 hours or until hen is tender. Or bake dressing in a buttered casserole dish at 350° F. until golden brown on top. This can be served as an entree, and you may use about a pound of ground venison, pork, or beef instead of the oysters. Serves 4–6.

7

Breads, Noodles, and Dumplings

Jack Lewis

Breads, Noodles, and Dumplings

If you ask a dozen Texans to give thanks for their daily bread, you can be sure that each has a different idea. Under any circumstances, from the rustic to the posh, every kind of meal calls for a special kind of bread. You'll want to remember some of these.

Betty Klein at the Sauer-Beckmann Living History Farm makes noodles the way her grandmother did.

Bill Reaves

What about this one for breakfast, or Sunday evening? The recipe is from Mrs. Annette Gragg of Houston, whom *Texas Highways* writer Howard Peacock proclaims "a fantastic cook."

Pecan Waffles

3 eggs, separated
2 cups buttermilk
2 cups flour
¼ teaspoon salt
2 teaspoons baking powder
1 teaspoon baking soda
6 tablespoons butter, melted
½ cup chopped pecans

Beat egg yolks until light. Add 1 cup of buttermilk, then sifted dry ingredients, and the remaining cup of buttermilk. Add melted butter and fold in beaten egg whites. Add pecans. Makes 4 large waffles.

To the really dedicated camper with a Dutch oven, sourdough biscuits won't be more difficult than anything else. This recipe, made from sourdough starter, was made public at Abilene's International Cowboy Campfire Cookoffs in the seventies. If you wear jeans, you can make the biscuits in the comfort of your own kitchen without losing your western frame of mind.

Sourdough Biscuits

2 cups flour, sifted
2 cups sourdough starter (recipe
  follows)
1 teaspoon salt
1 tablespoon sugar
2 heaping teaspoons baking powder
3 tablespoons shortening, melted and
  cooled

Put flour in a large bowl and make a hollow in it. Pour in sourdough starter and all other ingredients. Mix well into a soft dough. Pinch off egg-size pieces; place close together in a greased pan (or in a Dutch oven with cover for baking on an outdoor fire). Grease tops of biscuits. Let rise 5–10 minutes. Bake until brown in a hot oven (450° F.) or over coals, with more coals placed on top of lid.

Sourdough Starter

1 cake or envelope of dry yeast
4 cups warm water
2 tablespoons sugar
4 cups flour
1 raw potato, quartered

Dissolve yeast in warm water, and then mix all ingredients in a 1-gallon crock. (Do not use a metal container.) Cover with a close-fitting lid and let the starter rise until light (12 hours in warm weather, longer in cool weather). Do not let the starter get cold, ever. After using part of the starter, add 1 cup warm water, 2 teaspoons sugar, and enough flour to mix to the starter's original consistency. Add more potato occasionally as food for the yeast, but don't add more yeast. Use daily for best results. Starter improves with age.

When archaeologist Daphne Derven, wearing an authentic costume, recreated Christmas 1850 on the log cabin hearth at Old City Park in Dallas, she baked Indian bread in a Dutch oven on the side. Using an S-hook to lift the coal-covered lid requires some practice, but if you make the bread in your oven, you won't have to worry about spilling hot coals down your front. The recipe is easy.

Indian Bread with Buttermilk

4 cups buttermilk
1 teaspoon baking soda
2 tablespoons warm water
2 eggs, beaten
1 tablespoon melted butter or lard
1 teaspoon salt
cornmeal (8 cups or so)

Warm buttermilk slightly, and add baking soda dissolved in warm water. Stir and add well-beaten eggs, melted butter or lard, and a little salt. Using a spoon, stir in as much Indian cornmeal as will make a thick batter; beat it for a few minutes, pour into greased pans, and bake about 15 minutes at 450° F. Look at it often while baking, since it is liable to burn. Makes 3 loaves or cakes.

At one time, if you had asked for a recipe for biscuits, the cook would have said to dump some flour into a wooden bowl, make a well, then add shortening and liquid. If you had persisted in trying to record measurements, the amount of each would have been stated as "however much it takes." Besides, whatever biscuit recipe you use, the cream gravy is what counts. The following recipe, also from June Towers of Imperial Sugar, makes 24 biscuits . . . or enough for "2 cowhands or 12 computer programmers."

Hot Biscuits

2 cups all-purpose flour
1 tablespoon baking powder
¾ teaspoon salt
1 tablespoon granulated sugar
½ cup (1 stick) plus 2 tablespoons
    butter or margarine
2 eggs, well beaten
⅓ cup cold milk

Sift dry ingredients and cut in butter. Add well-beaten eggs and milk and mix lightly with fork. Shape into a ball of dough and roll out ½-inch thick. Fold dough in thirds and re-roll into an oblong two more times. Cut with a 2-inch biscuit cutter. Bake on ungreased baking sheets in a preheated 475° F. oven about 10 minutes or until biscuits are puffed and golden brown.

Cream Gravy

browned crumbs from a pan of
    sausage
3 tablespoons melted butter or
    margarine or drippings from
    sausage
¼ cup all-purpose flour
1 cup each of milk and water (more if
    necessary), heated
salt and pepper to taste

Stir flour into hot fat and sausage crumbs and cook until beginning to brown. Add hot milk and water, adding more if needed to thin. Taste for seasonings. Serves 6 office workers or 1 oil patch worker.

Phoebe Armstrong, who comes from a pioneer Big Thicket family, offers this version of East Texas sawmill cream gravy for biscuits:

Sawmill Gravy

You'll need ½ pound of sliced salt bacon, 3 tablespoons of flour, ½ cup of canned milk, and ½ cup of water. That's all. Mix the milk and water together. Wash and dry the salt bacon to remove excess fat. Fry it slowly in a large skillet to render the fat. When done, remove the bacon. Gradually add flour to the skillet, stirring constantly until it browns. Adjust the heat to keep the mixture barely bubbling; proper heat is critical. Add the liquid; keep on stirring. If too thick, thin with hot water. Taste before serving; add salt as needed. Spoon over hot biscuits, and garnish with crumbled bacon.

Thank Imperial Sugar for this relic from the past. These cinnamon rolls, according to June Towers of the Sugar Land company, were one reason our grandmothers were early to bed and early to rise. "First, they had to carry water into the house and make a fire in the wood-burning cooking range. The men of the household were already feeding the livestock and milking the cows. Foul weather or fair."

Cinnamon Rolls

1 cup scalded milk
¼ cup granulated sugar
1 teaspoon salt
¼ cup shortening
1 cake yeast (or 1 envelope dry yeast)
1 tablespoon lukewarm water for cake
    yeast (or very warm water for dry
    yeast)
1 egg, beaten
½ teaspoon lemon extract
½ teaspoon orange extract
2 cups all-purpose flour
    (approximately)
¾ cup granulated sugar
3 tablespoons melted butter
2 teaspoons cinnamon

Add sugar, salt, and shortening to scalded milk; cool. Add cake yeast to lukewarm water to dissolve (use very warm water for dry yeast). Then add beaten egg, extracts, and enough flour (about 2 cups) to make a dough that can be rolled out ½-inch thick. Divide dough into 3 parts. Roll out each part and spread with a mixture of the sugar, melted butter and cinnamon. Roll up like jelly roll and slice in 1-inch-thick slices. Place them in greased pan; let rise 45 minutes. Bake at 350° F. for 25 minutes or until golden brown.

Ramón Hartnett gave this one to *Texas Highways* from his home on the range:

Camp Bread

6 cups flour
1 teaspoon salt
1 teaspoon baking powder
1–1½ cups buttermilk
½ cup lard or shortening

Mix dry ingredients in large, shallow bowl. Add buttermilk slowly in center of flour mixture. Work in lard with fingers, using enough flour to form a soft ball. Grease a large cast-iron Dutch oven; pat dough out to fit in the bottom. Cover the Dutch oven and place over hot coals. Cook until golden brown (about 5 minutes). Depending on how hot the pan is, the time may vary.

Southern Spoon Bread

1 quart milk
2 cups cornmeal
1 teaspoon salt
3 tablespoons butter or margarine
3 eggs

Heat milk to boiling point. Stir in cornmeal, salt, and butter. Simmer 5 minutes. Cool. Separate eggs and beat yolks; add them to the cornmeal mixture. Fold in stiffly beaten egg whites. Pour batter into buttered casserole and bake at 350° F. 45 minutes, or until golden brown. Serve while hot in a cold glass of milk; eat with a spoon.

John Suhrstedt

3 cups flour
½ teaspoon salt
4 teaspoons baking powder
enough water to make a stiff dough

"Just before the dinner bell rings," writes Tommie Pinkard, "Eva pinches off small balls of dough, works them into about five-inch circles, and fries them in deep fat until they are a golden brown. Fry bread is best served hot with dripping butter, and is the perfect vehicle for transporting honey or cane syrup onto hungry palates."

It wouldn't be fair to deny the pioneers equal time for a bread recipe. In August 1979, Fayanne Teague recorded for posterity her old-fashioned recipes for hardtack, a simple cracker-type bread, and beef jerky to be eaten along with it. (See p. 32.) These are the genuine, original recipes that sustained her red-bearded great-great-great-grandfather, William Christmas Heard, his wife, Sarah Ann, and eight children on the journey westward.

"It would be the hardtack and jerky that would sustain them through their first winter in their new home," wrote Fayanne. "It would be more hardtack and jerky that 16 years later would nourish and sustain five of their seven sons through the Civil War. It would also be hardtack and jerky, prepared by Sarah Ann's recipe, that 128 years later would sustain their great-great-great-granddaughter on her modern-day pioneering backpacking excursions."

Basic Hardtack

2 cups flour
½ tablespoon salt (optional)
½ tablespoon sugar (optional)
½ cup water

Mix flour, salt (optional), sugar (optional), and water. Using hands or rolling pin, flatten dough on floured cloth until ¼-inch thick. Score with a knife if desired. Bake on cookie sheet in 350° F. oven for 30 minutes. Break into pieces as needed.

In October 1983, *Texas Highways* covered the annual reunion of the Anglo-Comanche Parker family, reviewing the story that began in 1836 with an Indian raid and the kidnapping of pioneer children. Indians and Anglos alike have been moved by the thought of Naduah, the blue-eyed Comanche squaw, who, upon hearing the name Parker among the white invaders, touched her chest and declared, "Cynthia Ann."

Married to the war chief Putak Nawkohnee (Nacona), Cynthia Ann gave birth to Quanah Parker, the last Comanche chief to retreat to the reservation in 1875.

Accompanying the story of the Parkers was a picture of women preparing Indian fry bread. When a reader asked for the recipe, it came out in the December issue "Letters," adapted by Mrs. Sandra Chesnut, a descendant of Quanah Parker.

Indian Fry Bread

2 cups self-rising flour
dash salt
2 tablespoons buttermilk
water
oil for frying

Mix ingredients, and add enough warm water to make a soft dough. Let it rest at least 1 hour. (When making big batches, let the dough sit overnight.) Break off golf-ball-size pieces, flatten each piece, and pat in your hands until it gets saucer size. Fry in hot, deep cooking oil until brown on both sides. Serves 6.

Eva Battise's Fry Bread

At Chief Fulton Battise's East Texas home on the Alabama-Coushatta Indian Reservation, where *Texas Highways* looked in for Thanksgiving in 1980, the fry bread was slightly different. The chief's wife, Eva, mixes:

73

Modern versions of hardtack (with sesame seeds) and jerky (with chili powder) fill out the saddlebag of a modern cowboy.

Modern Version of Hardtack

2 cups white flour
½ cup wheat germ
1 tablespoon sugar
2 cups *masa harina*
½ cup quick-cooking oats
1 tablespoon salt
sesame seeds (optional)
seasoned salt (optional)
caraway seeds (optional)
onion flakes (optional)
1½–1¾ cups water

Mix all dry ingredients thoroughly. Add water. Mix with hands until well moistened but not sticky. Divide into 4 parts, roll out each quarter until ¼-inch thick, place on cookie sheet (each part should cover half a cookie sheet). Bake in 350° F. oven for 30 minutes. Score with a knife before baking if desired. Break into pieces as needed. Keeps indefinitely in air-tight, moisture-proof containers. Zip-lock bags are good for carrying hardtack in a backpack.

They say that Cajuns of the Golden Triangle, Beaumont–Port Arthur–Orange, look to Louisiana as the "old country." According to Randy Mallory and Sallie Evans, oil-boom jobs brought thousands of Cajuns to Texas around the time of the Great Depression. With them, of course, came hot boudin (spicy pork and rice sausage), steaming crawfish, and their special *joie de vivre*. And of course, their coffee and

Beignets

2¼ cups flour
2 tablespoons sugar
⅛ teaspoon baking soda
1¼ cups milk
2 eggs, well beaten
1 teaspoon vanilla extract
deep fat for frying

Sift all dry ingredients into a mixing bowl. Combine milk, eggs, and vanilla. Stir into dry ingredients. Mix well. Drop by spoonfuls into deep hot fat and fry until golden brown. Drain on absorbent paper. Serve warm with butter and syrup (preferably ribbon cane). Makes 15–20 beignets.

Orange Nut Honey Bread

2 tablespoons shortening
1 cup honey
1 egg, beaten
1¼ tablespoons grated orange peel
2¼ cups flour, sifted
½ teaspoon soda
½ teaspoon salt
2½ teaspoons baking powder
¼ cup orange juice
¼ cup pecans, chopped

Cream shortening and honey together thoroughly. Add well-beaten egg and grated orange peel. Sift flour with other dry ingredients and add to creamed mixture alternately with the juice. Add nuts. Bake in greased loaf pan at 325° F. for 1 hour and 10 minutes. Serve with cream cheese softened with honey.

Some of the most colorful pictures in *Texas Highways* focus on community ethnic festivals, such as the Czech Fests, which fill the air with polka music and dancing in native Czech costume.

The Czechs began arriving in organized groups on Texas shores in 1852, bringing their traditional violins and folk dances from Moravia and Bohemia. Like most of our turmoil-fleeing ancestors, they came seeking peace and the opportunity to work hard for a better life. Encouraged by glowing letters from a clergyman-farmer, Arnosty Bergmann, they came to the Gulf Coast area, where Czech manpower already had built much of the railroad west of Galveston.

One of the first and best Czech festivals, sponsored by the Rosenberg-Richmond Chamber of Commerce of Fort Bend County, draws a mixed crowd from miles around. The food may have something to do with that. An apocryphal sort of story holds that in 1978, when Bum Phillips, who was Houston Oilers coach then, came to judge the kolache-baking contest, he offered to trade two draft choices for a second *klobasniky*. For the untutored in Czech delights, *klobasniky* are foot-long sausages encased in airy kolache dough, and served piping hot with a dollop of mustard.

Texas Highways can't resist trying ethnic recipes, such as:

Kolaches

Yeast Starter

5 teaspoons dry yeast
½ cup warm milk
2 tablespoons sugar
½ cup flour

Dissolve yeast in warm milk; add sugar and flour and mix well. Cover and set aside to rise about 10 minutes.

Dough

½ cup butter
2 eggs, separated
1 pint cream
grated rind of 1 lemon
1½ teaspoons salt
6 cups sifted flour (approximate)

Cream butter; add egg yolks one at a time. Add yeast starter, beaten egg whites, cream, lemon rind, salt, and flour. Work dough with a spoon until spoon stays clean of flour, about 30 minutes. Set aside to rise to double in size (about 1 hour).

Cut off tablespoon-size pieces of dough and shape slightly flattened balls. (At this stage, surplus kolaches may be placed on a tray and frozen. See note below.) Place on greased baking pan. Make a shallow dent; add filling and crumb topping. Let rise again and bake at 375–400° F. 20 minutes or until done. Makes 5 dozen.

Cottage Cheese Filling

1 cup drained cottage cheese (must be dry)
2 tablespoons flour
½ cup sugar or more to taste
¼–½ teaspoon nutmeg
raisins if desired

Mix all ingredients.

Dried Fruit Filling

1 pound dried prunes or apricots
½ cup water
½ cup sugar
**cinnamon and grated lemon rind to
    taste (for prunes)**
**nutmeg and ginger to taste (for
    apricots)**

Combine dried fruit and water. Cook
over low heat until tender. Mash up
fruit (pit prunes) and sweeten with
sugar. To prunes, add cinnamon and
grated lemon rind. To apricots, add
nutmeg and ginger.

Crumb Topping

¾ cup sugar
½ cup flour
3 tablespoons melted butter

Combine sugar, flour, and melted butter. Work with fingers until crumbly.
Sprinkle on top of fruit filling.

Note: If you don't need 5 dozen, after
shaping kolaches (before filling) freeze
quickly on a tray, then store in a plastic bag. When ready to bake them,
place kolaches on a buttered pan to
thaw, and continue the recipe.

Here's the cornbread to go with
your hambone soup or collard
greens. The U.T. Institute of Texan
Cultures recommends it.

Cornbread

2 cups buttermilk
2 eggs
1 teaspoon baking soda
2 cups yellow cornmeal
2 tablespoons sugar (optional)
1 teaspoon salt
1 teaspoon melted butter
drop of vanilla

Combine buttermilk, eggs, and soda
and beat well. Sift together cornmeal,
sugar, and salt. Add buttermilk mixture, butter, and vanilla, and mix well.
Pour in a buttered baking pan. Bake at
450° F. Makes 8–10 servings.

Easter eggs with traditional Wendish designs

When you make Polish *barscz* you'll
want to make these filled dumplings
to have with it. They came to us
from *The Melting Pot.*

Uszka

Wrapping

2 cups flour
1 egg
1 cup water
½ teaspoon salt
2 tablespoons mashed potatoes

Mound flour on kneading board. Beat
egg slightly with water and salt. Pour
carefully in mound of flour. Mix and add
potatoes. Knead until dough becomes
elastic. Cover closely with a warm bowl
and let stand about 10 minutes.

    For easier handling, divide dough in
half. Roll out very thin, and cut in 2-
inch squares. Place ½ teaspoon of filling a little to one side of each square.
Moisten edge with water, fold over, and
press edges together. Join two upper
corners. Drop into salted boiling water
and cook until they float to top. Serves 4.

Meatless Filling

2 tablespoons chopped onion
3 tablespoons butter
**2 cups mushrooms, cooked and
    chopped**
salt and pepper

To prepare filling: Sauté onion in butter
until light brown. Add mushrooms and
sauté very slowly for 10 minutes. Add
salt and pepper and cool.

Another ethnic recipe from *The
Melting Pot:*

Wendish Noodles

3 eggs
2 tablespoons water
½ teaspoon salt
2½ cups flour
4 cups chicken or beef stock
2 tablespoons butter or margarine
1 tablespoon parsley, chopped
**1 tablespoon green onion tops,
    chopped**
dash nutmeg

Beat eggs; add water, salt, and about
2¼ cups flour to make a stiff dough. Let
stand for 10–20 minutes. Make five
balls of dough and roll them very thin,
using the rest of flour. Let dry on the
table until they will not stick together
when stacked. Cut into 2-inch strips,
stack, and cut to desired width with a
very sharp knife. Cook 3 cups of noodles
in 4 cups boiling chicken or beef stock.
Boil noodles for 10 minutes or longer,
but do not overboil. Add 2 tablespoons
butter or margarine. Chopped parsley,
chopped green onion tops, and a dash
of nutmeg may be added for flavor.

8

Desserts

Karen Dickey-Johnson/TDA

Cakes, Pastries, and Fruit

Jack L

How sweet it would be for pioneer merchant and banker Samuel May Williams to feast his eyes on Sugar Land. In 1843, he built a small cane mill called Imperial Sugar Company. At the time, Williams never pictured soft, snow-white powders and granules, or calibrated shades of moist brown sugars. He never would have dreamed of tankcars of industrial liquid sugar. Of course, now that *Texas Highways* has looked into and told us about Sugar Land, the biggest gain is ours . . . although it may be only a matter of inches . . . around the middle!

Pursuing a tradition of publishing recipes, the company published a book called *Romantic Recipes of the Old South*. The Daughters of the American Revolution collected old recipes for the project, throwing in stories and legends for extra flavor. Your grandmother probably baked the blackberry jam cake, one of those Romantic Recipes.

East Texas Blueberries flavor a delightful cream cake.

Blackberry Jam Cake

1 cup shortening
2 cups granulated sugar
4 egg yolks, beaten
1 teaspoon vanilla
3 cups sifted flour
1 teaspoon soda
2 teaspoons cinnamon
1 teaspoon nutmeg
1 teaspoon ground cloves
1 teaspoon allspice
1 cup buttermilk
1 cup blackberry jam
4 egg whites, beaten

Cream shortening and sugar together until light. Add beaten egg yolks and vanilla. Beat until thoroughly blended. Sift dry ingredients together and add alternately with buttermilk. Stir in blackberry jam. Fold in beaten egg whites. Pour batter into 10-inch tube pan which has been lined on bottom with waxed paper and greased. Bake in preheated 325° F. oven for 30 minutes; increase heat to 350° F. and continue baking for about 45 minutes or until cake tests done. Set pan on wire rack and allow cake to cool 20 minutes before removing from pan.

If you think that rabbiteyes are just for seeking out lettuce and carrots, look what Sam Garner found at Fincastle Farms: sweet, succulent rabbiteye blueberries. Only a few years ago, a new Southern strain of this luscious Yankee fruit was imported to Texas from Georgia by John Schoellkopf of Fincastle. By 1983, people were coming from throughout East Texas and beyond to pick their own berries and to buy plants and jellies. When you get yours, try them fresh with cantaloupe first (see p. 82) and make cookies, cake, or pie with the next batch.

Use fresh or dry-pack frozen blueberries in these recipes. If you use sweetened berries, you will have to adjust the sugar in the recipe.

Blueberries are highly perishable at room temperature, but you can store fresh, dry blueberries up to two weeks in the refrigerator. Do not wash them until you are ready to use them because wet ones will mold.

Blueberry Cream Cake

2 white cake layers (standard cake mix or favorite recipe)

Glaze and Topping

1 cup sugar
1 tablespoon cornstarch
1 cup water
2 cups blueberries (sliced strawberries may be substituted for ½ of the cup used for topping)

Mix sugar and cornstarch; blend in water and ½ cup mashed blueberries. (Reserve 1½ cups.) Cook over medium heat, stirring constantly, until mixture thickens and comes to a boil. Continue to stir and cook 2 minutes, until mixture is clear. Strain and set aside to cool.

Icing

2 tablespoons butter or margarine
3 ounces cream cheese
3–4 cups powdered sugar
1 teaspoon vanilla flavoring
1 cup whipping cream, whipped

Cream butter and cheese. Add powdered sugar and vanilla. (Use more than 3 cups of sugar if needed for a firm icing.) Fold in whipped cream.

Assembly

Spread icing between layers, on top and sides of cake. Reserve ½ cup blueberries for garnish and pile remaining 1 cup in center of cake. Pour cooled glaze over fruit. Arrange reserved blueberries around sides. Chill until serving time.

Adapted from Mary Faulk Koock's Christmas favorites:

Lady Baltimore Cake

1 cup butter
2 cups sugar
4 eggs, separated
1 cup milk
3 cups flour
4 teaspoons baking powder
½ teaspoon salt
1 teaspoon vanilla or almond extract

Cream butter and sugar together. Add beaten egg yolks, then the milk alternately with sifted dry ingredients. Add extract and fold in beaten egg whites. Bake in two 9-inch greased cake pans at 350° F. for 35–40 minutes.

Filling and Icing

1½ cups sugar
¼ teaspoon cream of tartar
¼ teaspoon salt
⅓ cup cold water
2 egg whites, beaten
½ teaspoon almond or vanilla extract
½ cup raisins, chopped
½ cup walnuts, chopped
6 dried light figs, finely cut
6 dates, pitted and chopped
6 candied cherries, chopped

Mix the first four ingredients; stir until sugar dissolves. Cook on low heat until syrup dropped from a spoon will spin a thread, or reaches 240° F. on a candy thermometer. (Keep covered and do not stir while cooking.) Pour syrup gradually over beaten egg whites, beating all the while until mixture stands in peaks. Add flavoring and reserve one-third of icing for sides of cake. Add chopped fruits and nuts to remaining two-thirds of icing. Spread on top of cooled cake layers as filling and icing, then frost sides of layers with plain frosting.

Note: The original cake recipe included twice this amount of fruit and nuts in the frosting, which is very rich and delicious. Unless, however, you expect to use the whole layer cake the first day, the frosting might give way on the sides. The original recipe would be fine on a single 9-by-13-inch layer.

Texas Highways considered naming this cheesecake our unofficial state dessert. It's good enough at the sour cream level, but it lends itself to seasonal toppings. In the summer, strawberries shimmer beneath a glaze. In the winter, a luscious topping can be made from canned blueberries. Canned peaches, drained and soaked in sherry, can be placed in a pattern on the sour cream layer before baking. Chocolate enthusiasts fold six ounces of tiny semisweet bits into the batter, and then, after baking the sour cream layer into place, scatter driblets of melted bitter chocolate over the top. If time runs out, simply use a canned fruit-pie filling for topping.

Sovereign State Cheesecake

Crust

6 tablespoons butter
1⅓ cups graham cracker crumbs
½ cup sugar

Melt butter, remove from heat, and stir in crumbs and sugar with a fork until well mixed. Press a layer of the mixture on the bottom and halfway up the sides of a 10-inch springform pan. Bake 5 minutes at 350° F. or refrigerate while making the filling.

Note: Be careful to cover the entire surface of pan to prevent holes in the crust.

Filling

4 extra large eggs
¾ cup sugar
2 8-ounce packages cream cheese, softened
1 teaspoon vanilla

Beat eggs, add sugar, and continue beating until light yellow and fluffy. Break off bits of soft cream cheese and add to the mixture. Mix in vanilla and beat until cream cheese is dissolved and filling is smooth. Pour carefully into the crust and bake at 375° F. for 35 minutes. Top will start to look firm and dry, but not scorched.

Sour Cream Layer

1 cup sour cream
3 tablespoons sugar
½ teaspoon vanilla

© Donald Wristen

Sovereign State Cheesecake, with red, white, or blue topping

Move oven setting up to 450° F. Beat sour cream with sugar and vanilla. Spread over filling. Bake 5 minutes. Cool cheesecake completely before chilling or adding any extra topping. Store in refrigerator. Serves 8.

Blueberry Glaze

14-ounce can blueberries, plus ¾ cup juice
¼ cup sugar
1½ tablespoons cornstarch
1 teaspoon butter

Reserve ¾ cup juice from blueberries, or, if necessary, add water to total ¾ cup liquid. Stir liquid in saucepan with sugar and cornstarch over medium heat until mixture starts to thicken. Add blueberries and stir carefully with wooden spoon 2 minutes. Stir in butter and cool slightly. Spoon topping over cheesecake and chill.

Strawberry Topping

1 quart fresh strawberries
¾ cup sugar
1½ tablespoons cornstarch
¼ cup water
dash salt
1 teaspoon butter
3–4 drops red food coloring

Wash and hull strawberries. Crush 1 cup of uneven-sized berries and set aside remainder. In a small saucepan, combine crushed berries, sugar, cornstarch, water, and salt. Cook over medium heat, stirring constantly until thickened. Cook 2 minutes more, stirring constantly. Remove from heat, and stir in butter and food coloring. Put through a strainer, and allow to cool slightly. Arrange whole berries on top of cheesecake and spoon glaze over to cover evenly. Chill.

Note: For extra generous topping, make the recipe using half again the amount of each ingredient, and cook an extra minute.

80

In 1983, this recipe for carrot teacake was given to me by Jean Louis Kippelen (then at Inn on the Park in Houston), and was published in *Texas Highways* with teatime treats from the Adolphus Hotel in Dallas.

Carrot Teacake

2 cups sifted, all-purpose flour
½ teaspoon baking powder
⅛ teaspoon (scant) baking soda
⅛ teaspoon ground cinnamon
1 pinch salt
1½ cups vegetable oil
2 cups sugar
3 whole eggs
½ cup crushed pineapple, drained
1 cup finely chopped walnuts
3 cups shredded carrots

Preheat oven to 350° F. Sift flour, baking powder, soda, cinnamon, and salt together and set aside. Combine oil and sugar in a large mixing bowl, beating until well mixed. Add sifted ingredients and continue mixing, scraping the side of the bowl with a rubber spatula. Add whole eggs, one at a time until well blended. Do not overmix. Stir in pineapple, walnuts, and carrots. Grease 2 4-by-8-inch loaf pans, and fill half full. Bake 40–45 minutes, or until a toothpick inserted in the center comes out clean.

A persimmon favorite from the magazine:

Persimmon Cake

½ cup shortening or other fat
1 cup sugar
1 cup persimmon puree (follows)
2 eggs, beaten
2 cups sifted flour
½ teaspoon baking soda
3 teaspoons baking powder

Cream fat and sugar together; add the puree and eggs. Sift the dry ingredients and add to the persimmon mixture. Beat well, pour into a greased baking pan, and bake at 350° F. about 1 hour.

Puree

Sort, wash, and peel persimmons and cut in sections. Press through a sieve or process in a blender. Mix in ⅛ teaspoon crystalline ascorbic acid or 1½ teaspoons crystalline citric acid with each quart of puree. Seal and freeze any puree not used immediately.

Texas Highways celebrated the pecan tree in 1986, in a salute from writer Howard Peacock to the state tree of Texas. Who ever has too many pecan recipes? Even if you do, try this one. It's a semisweet cake from Doretta Gilchrist of Woodville, Texas.

Pecan Whiskey Cake

2 cups flour
2 teaspoons baking powder
½ cup butter, softened
1 cup sugar
4 eggs
½ teaspoon nutmeg (grated fresh is better)
1 teaspoon cinnamon
½ teaspoon salt
½ cup whiskey
1 cup raisins, chopped
2 cups pecans

Blend flour and baking powder; reserve ¼ cup and set aside. Cream butter and sugar until fluffy and beat in eggs. Add nutmeg, cinnamon, and salt. Blend in whiskey and flour alternately in small increments, mixing well after each addition. Combine raisins and pecans with reserved flour, then blend into batter. Pour into greased and floured 8-inch square pan. Bake at 325° F. about 1 hour. Test with toothpick. Cool in pan and cut in squares, or cut into thirds, slicing each rectangle into thin slices.

Mrs. Meta Mund, a champion blue-ribbon winner from Fredericksburg says this one "always turns out good":

Blue-Ribbon Cocoa Divinity Cake

1½ cups sugar
⅔ cup vegetable shortening
2 eggs
1 teaspoon vanilla
1 cup sour milk* or buttermilk
2 cups sifted flour
½ teaspoon baking soda
1½ teaspoons baking powder
½ teaspoon salt
6 tablespoons cocoa

*Add 1 tablespoon lemon juice or white vinegar to 1 cup sweet milk to make it sour.

Cream first four ingredients. Blend in milk and sifted dry ingredients alternately. Bake in 2 greased and floured 9-inch round cake pans about 30 minutes at 350° F. Frost with confectioners' sugar frosting flavored with vanilla.

Texas Peach Kuchen

6 medium Texas peaches
2 tablespoons lemon juice
1½ cups flour
2 teaspoons baking powder
½ cup sugar
½ teaspoon salt
2 eggs
2 tablespoons milk
1½ teaspoons grated lemon peel
¼ cup butter, melted
¼ cup sugar
½ teaspoon cinnamon
1 egg yolk
3 tablespoons whipping cream

Peel and slice peaches; pour on lemon juice. Sift the next four ingredients onto waxed paper. Combine and beat with a fork 2 eggs, milk, lemon peel. Add flour mixture and melted butter. Pour into a buttered 9-inch springform pan or a 9-inch round baking pan (plan to serve from this pan). Drain peach slices and arrange on the batter. Sprinkle evenly over the peaches the ¼ cup sugar and cinnamon. Bake at 400° F. about 25 minutes. Remove from the oven and pour on a mixture of the egg yolk beaten with whipping cream.

These two oldies are from Christmas 1850, recreated in 1984 by Daphne Derven. Still good, after all these years. (Use ½ teaspoon of almond or vanilla flavoring instead of lemon cordial.) For a historically more accurate texture, Daphne substitutes ¼ cup whole wheat flour for ¼ cup white flour in these recipes.

Almond (or Pecan) Cake

Cream 1 pound of sugar with ½ pound butter. Add 4 eggs, one at a time, and ½ teaspoon of baking soda, ½ of a grated nutmeg, and 1 tablespoon lemon cordial. Add ¼ pound chopped almonds (or pecans) and 2 cups of flour, or as needed to make a stiff batter. Bake at 350° F. for 30 minutes.

Ginger Cakes

To 2–3 cups flour and 1 cup brown or raw sugar add 1 cup butter, 2 large spoonfuls of ginger, a grated nutmeg, and 1 cup cane syrup or molasses. Mix together, moisten with cream; batter should be stiff. Roll out and cut into little cakes. Bake on tin plates (or in muffin tins) at 325° F., until brown at the edges.

This is the Lebanese version of the Greek *baklava*:

Janie Ashmore's Behlawa (Layered Dessert)

Syrup

3 cups sugar
2¼ cups water
1 teaspoon orange water (optional)
2 tablespoons lemon juice

Make syrup by boiling sugar and water in a saucepan until it registers 229° F. on a candy thermometer. Add orange water and lemon juice and remove the pan from heat. Cool and strain.

1 pound drawn butter
1 pound pecans
4 tablespoons sugar
1 tablespoon butter
1 teaspoon orange water (optional)
1 pound phyllo pastry sheets thawed
  (about 20 sheets)

Prepare drawn butter: Melt 1 pound butter slowly over lowest flame possible about 1 hour, or until it becomes clear. As it melts, skim all white foam (salt) from the top carefully. Do not let the butter become brown. Strain and allow to cool.

Grind pecans and mix with sugar and 1 tablespoon butter; add orange water. Brush a 10-by-13-inch baking pan with drawn butter. Brush each sheet of phyllo with drawn butter and layer one on top of the other.

Halfway through, instead of buttering the phyllo sheet, spread the nut mixture in a thick layer. Then continue layering buttered phyllo over the filling. Top with two sheets that have no butter between them, and brush the top with butter. Score diagonally into diamonds, each with four 2-inch sides. Preheat oven to 350° F., then lower to 250° F. Bake 1½–2 hours, or until light golden brown. Remove from the oven and drizzle 2 cups of cool syrup slowly to saturate pastry, especially over the scoring. When cool, finish cutting into serving-size pieces. Makes about 3 dozen pieces.

From "Bonnie's Home Cooking," *Texas Highways*, February 1978:

Bananas Foster

1 tablespoon butter
2 tablespoons brown sugar
1 ripe banana
dash cinnamon
½ ounce banana liqueur
1 ounce white rum

Melt butter in chafing dish. Add brown sugar and blend well. Peel and slice banana lengthwise and sauté in butter and sugar. Sprinkle with cinnamon. Pour liqueur and rum over banana, and ignite. Baste banana with flaming liquid. Serve when flame dies (alcohol will have oxidized). It's great with ice cream.

Just across the tracks from the Texas and Pacific station in Marshall, in 1896, Ginocchio's Hotel was built, with a foundation of big solid beams spaced at 12-inch intervals on 3½-foot-thick stone blocks.

During 80 years of rumbling trains, the old place never even rattled.

"About the time incandescent light bulbs came into use, a representative of Mr. Edison came through Marshall," says owner and restaurateur Sam Litzenberg. "He sold the system to Ginocchio and installed it here. The lights were powered by a wet cell battery in the base of the center post in the lobby. They were the first electric lights in the Southwest. But Ginocchio didn't take any chances; he had gas jets built in just in case something happened to his new-fangled lights."

Litzenberg no longer operates a restaurant on that site, but you can make his pet dessert at home.

Glory Hallelujah

1½ cups crumbled macaroons
½ cup sugar
½ cup Cognac or Tía María
1 pint whipping cream, whipped stiff

Blend the macaroons, sugar, and Cognac. Fold in whipped cream, and place mixture in individual dessert or custard cups. Freeze for at least 3 hours. Mixture will stiffen, but not freeze. Serves 8.

Adapted from recipes of the 1850s:

Daphne Derven's Baked Pears

Pare, but leave the stems on, 7 pears. Put in a deep, 10-inch baking dish with ½ pound of brown sugar or molasses and a grated lemon rind. Cover the bottom of the dish with brandy and bake in a 350° F. oven until tender, about 1 hour. Glaze each pear with 1 tablespoon grape jelly.

Berry-Filled Cantaloupe

3 cantaloupes, chilled
4 cups blueberries
½ cup grenadine
2 tablespoons lemon juice
6 tablespoons sifted powdered sugar

Cut melons into halves. Remove seeds. Combine rest of ingredients, and pile mixture lightly in the cantaloupe cavities. Chill. Serves 6.

Rum cake, served at Brent Place at Old City Park in Dallas, is adapted from an old Texas farm recipe. It is offered with wassail to Christmas visitors.

The old Brent House at Plano had been standing for nearly 100 years when the Dallas Heritage Society moved it to Old City Park. The house was rebuilt from old materials for authenticity, even to replacement of old shutters and screens with still older glass.

Rum Cake

½ **cup finely chopped pecans**
1 **box butter cake mix for 2-layer cake**
1 **package (not instant) vanilla**
  pudding mix (4-serving size)
4 **eggs, beaten**
½ **cup light rum**
½ **cup cooking oil**
½ **cup water**

Preheat oven to 325° F. Grease and flour Bundt pan. In bottom of pan, sprinkle ½ cup finely chopped pecans. Combine cake mix with pudding mix; add beaten eggs, rum, oil, and water, and blend thoroughly. Pour into pan over pecans. Bake about 1 hour. Remove from oven, and while still hot, drizzle rum glaze (see below) over cake. Leave in pan for at least 30 minutes so the glaze can soak through the cake.

Rum Glaze

1 **stick (¼ pound) butter**
1 **cup sugar**
¼ **cup light rum**
¼ **cup water**

Blend all ingredients, bring to a boil, and boil 2–3 minutes.

———————————

Peaches and Texas knew each other when. Spaniards planted peach trees at their missions in the sixteenth century. Surprisingly some offshoots of these, growing semi-wild, still exist.

At one time, East Texas Elberta peaches from some 15 million trees boosted Texas to the position of the nation's biggest producer. But

growing peaches always presents a challenge. The golden fruit depends on specific environmental chilling factors and exactly the right soil.

Most of us need only enjoy the fruit. Treat yourself to fresh peaches. Make Mrs. Lyndon B. Johnson's peach ice cream, below or Texas peach kuchen (p. 81).

A word of advice from *Texas Highways'* Tommie Pinkard: Peel peaches carefully, the way you do tomatoes. Bring a pot of water to the boil and put in peaches for 1 minute. Then rinse under cold water and slip off the skin.

Mrs. Lyndon B. Johnson's Peach Ice Cream

1 **quart whipping cream**
1 **pint milk**
3 **Texas eggs**
1 **cup sugar**
½ **gallon soft Texas peaches, mashed**
  and sweetened to taste

Make a boiled custard of the cream, milk, eggs, and sugar. Cool and add the peaches, mashed and well sweetened. Freeze in a 1-gallon ice cream freezer.

———————————

The next time the jagged edge of your grapefruit spoon slashes into a Texas Ruby Red, give thanks for small favors. The Rio Grande Val-

ley's billion-dollar citrus industry began with a single orange from the saddlebag of an itinerant Catholic priest. Seven trees grew from the seeds he planted a century ago. A vision of the fruits of his labor might have inspired a strong homily.

Celebrate prosperity with this orange soufflé from Regis Dernard, assistant pastry chef at Inn on the Park in Houston.

Orange Soufflé with Grand Marnier Sauce

7 **egg yolks (divided 3 + 4)**
½ **cup plus 1 tablespoon sugar**
1 **cup cake flour**
2 **cups milk**
juice of 2 oranges (about 6 ounces)
½ **cup Grand Marnier liqueur**
4 **egg whites**
1 **extra tablespoon sugar for egg**
  whites

Mix 3 egg yolks with sugar and stir in flour. Add ½ cup of milk to the egg yolk base. Bring remaining milk to a boil and add to the egg mixture. Cook until base is a thick paste (2–3 minutes). Refrigerate the base until it is cold. After base is cold, add remaining 4 egg yolks. Combine orange juice and Grand Marnier, and add to base. Whip egg whites, slowly adding 1 tablespoon of sugar. Do not overwhip; the egg whites should be light. Fold into the base mixture. Place in a 2-quart soufflé dish. Bake at 400° F. for 20–22 minutes. Serves 4.

Puddin' and Pie

Pucker up, again! Now, how long has it been since you enjoyed a good persimmon? Actually, freezing takes the pucker out and gives uniformity to persimmons that are at different stages of ripeness, according to the Texas Agricultural Extension Service. Or add ½ teaspoon of soda to 1 cup of persimmon pulp before it is heated. And please, keep the color nice by cooking it in something other than tin or iron.

Rice Council of America

Soft Rice Custard with Peach Topping

Texas Highways has found all the best ways to have persimmons. Try them in pudding, courtesy of Mrs. Ronald Reagan, or custard, courtesy of the Texas A&M System.

Mrs. Reagan's Recipe for Persimmon Pudding

1 cup sugar
½ cup melted butter
1 cup flour, sifted
¼ teaspoon salt
1 teaspoon cinnamon
¼ teaspoon nutmeg
1 cup persimmon pulp (3 or 4 very ripe persimmons)
2 teaspoons baking soda
2 teaspoons warm water
3 tablespoons brandy
1 teaspoon vanilla
2 eggs, slightly beaten
1 cup seedless raisins
½ cup walnuts, chopped (optional)

Stir together sugar and melted butter. Resift flour with salt, cinnamon, and nutmeg, and add to butter mixtures. Add persimmon pulp, soda dissolved in warm water, brandy, and vanilla. Add eggs, mixing thoroughly but lightly. Add raisins and nuts, stirring until mixed. Put in buttered steam-type covered mold and steam 2½ hours. Flame at table with brandy. Serve with brandy whipped cream sauce.

Brandy Whipped Cream Sauce

1 egg
⅓ cup melted butter
1 cup sifted powdered sugar
dash of salt
1 tablespoon brandy flavoring
1 cup whipping cream

Beat egg until light and fluffy. Beat in butter, powdered sugar, salt, and brandy flavoring. Beat whipping cream until stiff. Gently fold into first mixture. Cover and chill until ready to serve. Stir before spooning on pudding.

Persimmon Custard

2 cups persimmon puree (see Persimmon Cake, p. 81)
½ cup sugar
1 teaspoon baking soda
⅛ teaspoon nutmeg
¼ teaspoon cinnamon
2 eggs, separated
1/16 teaspoon salt
¼ cup sugar

Combine puree with next four ingredients and 2 beaten egg yolks. Pour into a baking dish. Place in a pan of hot water and bake at 300° F. about 15 minutes. Make a meringue using the salt, egg whites, and ¼ cup sugar. Put on top of the custard, and bake at 300° F. until custard is lightly browned. Makes 4–6 servings.

The dessert below is for the calorie conscious:

Orange Yogurt Whip

2 packages unflavored gelatin
1 cup boiling water
1 cup orange juice
1½ cups lowfat yogurt, unflavored
3 orange slices, or other fruit

Dissolve gelatin in boiling water. Pour in orange juice. Chill until mixture is almost set. Beat until fluffy; add yogurt. Pour into individual glasses. Garnish with fruit. Makes 3 servings.

Imperial Sweet Potato Pudding

1 egg
2 cups milk
3 cups grated raw sweet potatoes
4 tablespoons butter, melted
2 cups brown sugar
½ teaspoon cinnamon
¼ teaspoon cloves
¼ teaspoon allspice
¼ teaspoon salt

Beat egg slightly; add remaining ingredients and mix well. Pour into a buttered 1½-quart baking dish. Bake in a preheated 325° F. oven for 45 minutes or until well browned, stirring occasionally. Serves 8.

Another good thing to do with East Texas long grain rice:

Soft Rice Custard with Peach Topping

3 cups cooked rice
4 cups milk
⅔ cup sugar
¾ teaspoon salt
2 eggs, beaten
2 tablespoons butter or margarine
1 teaspoon vanilla extract

Combine rice, 3½ cups milk, sugar, and salt. Cook over medium heat, stirring occasionally, until it comes to a boil and is thick and creamy (about 15 minutes). Blend remaining ½ cup milk and eggs. Stir into rice mixture. Cook 2 minutes longer, stirring constantly. Add butter and vanilla. Turn into serving dishes. Serve warm or cold with peach topping, below. Makes 6–8 servings.

Peach Topping

¼ cup brown sugar
2 teaspoons cornstarch
¼ teaspoon salt
½ teaspoon cinnamon
16-ounce can sliced peaches
1 tablespoon butter or margarine
2 tablespoons brandy or 1 teaspoon brandy extract

Blend first five ingredients. Cook, stirring constantly, over low heat until thickened. Remove from heat; add butter and brandy. Cool.

Here's an outdoor pudding from cowpuncher Ramón Hartnett's range in West Texas. If you aren't a camper, you can make it on the range in your kitchen.

Rice Pudding

8 cups water
¼ teaspoon salt
4 cups uncooked rice
2 cups sugar
12-ounce can evaporated milk
4 teaspoons vanilla
15-ounce box of raisins

Bring water and salt to boil in large skillet over hot coals. Add rice, cover, and cook. When done, add rest of ingredients to rice. Heat, stirring frequently.

Brent House Apple Mincemeat Cobbler

2 cups apple pie filling
2 cups mincemeat
¼ cup lemon juice
1 cup brown sugar
2 teaspoons cinnamon
1 teaspoon nutmeg
⅓ cup butter
brandy or rum to taste

Combine all ingredients and place in 9-by-13-inch pan. Top with cobbler crust (below). Bake at 375° F. for 30 minutes or until filling is hot and bubbly and crust is brown.

Cobbler Crust

2 cups biscuit mix
¼ pound soft butter (not melted)
6 tablespoons boiling water

Put biscuit mix in bowl with soft butter. Pour in boiling water. Mix with a fork till mixture forms a ball. Grease hands and pat out piece of dough. Place over fruit and mincemeat.

Fincastle Blueberry Pie

1 baked 9-inch pastry shell
1 package (4-serving size) vanilla pudding and pie filling mix (non-instant)
1¾ cups milk
½ cup whipping cream, whipped
2 cups blueberries
1 cup flaked coconut

Prepare pie filling according to package directions, but use only 1¾ cups milk. Cover and cool. Fold whipped cream and 1½ cups blueberries into the filling. Spoon into pie shell and cover with remaining berries. Sprinkle coconut over the berries. Chill.

Fresh Grapefruit Pie

3 or 4 Ruby Red grapefruit (divided)
2 packages unflavored gelatin
2 eggs separated
½ cup plus 2 tablespoons sugar
⅛ teaspoon salt
8-ounce package cream cheese, softened
1 cup sour cream
3 drops red food coloring (optional)
1 baked 9-inch pie shell
Maraschino cherries

Peel and section one grapefruit. Carefully remove membrane; set sections aside for garnish. Halve and juice the remaining fruit. Strain juice; measure 1½ cups. In small saucepan, soften gelatin in ½ cup juice, then dissolve over low heat. Set aside. Pour remaining cup of juice in blender container. Add egg yolks, ½ cup sugar, salt, cream cheese, sour cream, and food coloring. Whirl smooth. Add dissolved gelatin and blend 5 seconds more. Chill until slightly thickened. Beat egg whites with 2 tablespoons sugar until stiff. Fold egg whites into gelatin mixture. Pour into pie shell and chill until firm. Garnish with grapefruit sections and cherries.

Texas Buttermilk Pie

1⅞ cup sugar
4 tablespoons flour
½ cup butter, melted and cooled
3 eggs, beaten
1 cup buttermilk
1 teaspoon vanilla
dash of nutmeg (optional)
unbaked 9-inch pie shell

Preheat oven to 425° F. Mix sugar and flour together until fine. Add cooled butter, beaten eggs, buttermilk, vanilla, and nutmeg if desired. Mix and pour into pie shell. Bake 10 minutes at 425° F.; turn temperature down to 350° F. and continue to bake until the pie sets, about 40 minutes. Cool on rack; do not cut while hot.

For Christmas 1975, *Texas Highways* located the state's all-round, all-time, unmatched cooking champion to share her favorite blue-ribbon recipes. Mrs. Meta Mund lived in a little house near Fredericksburg in the middle of 40 acres of land . . . and about 40 acres of ribbons. In 1975 alone, Mrs. Mund took 41 entries to the Gillespie County Fair. She received 33 blue ribbons and 8 second-place citations.

Meta Mund's Instant Chocolate Cream Pie

Mix 1 small package instant chocolate pudding with 1 cup milk. Add 1 cup of whipping cream that has been whipped. Pour into baked pie shell and chill. Serve with more whipped cream.

The following recipe is reprinted from *Feasting Free on Wild Edibles*, with permission from Stackpole Books.

Bradford Angier's Elderberry Pie

4 cups dried berries, mixed with a little water
4 tablespoons flour
1½ cups sugar
4 tablespoons butter, melted
pastry for double-crust pie

Stew berries with a little water and measure out 4 cups. Thicken with the flour; add sugar (more or less to taste) and melted butter. Pour into pie shell. Make strips with remaining pastry and crisscross over the pie filling.

Bake in the oven at 350° F. 1 hour or until pastry turns brown.

Strawberry Tarts, favorites during teatime at Dallas' Hotel Adolphus

Another pecan recipe from *Texas Highways* and Mrs. Annette Gragg:

Pecan Tarts (Texas Tassies)

Pastry

2 sticks (½ pound) margarine
2 3-ounce packages cream cheese
2 cups flour

Combine and press into small size muffin tins to form crust.

Filling

2 cups brown sugar
2 eggs
2 tablespoons margarine, melted
¼ teaspoon salt
1 teaspoon vanilla
1 cup chopped pecans

Combine all ingredients of filling; mix well. Pour into unbaked crusts and bake in a 350° F. oven for 15 minutes. Then turn oven to 250° F. and continue baking for 10 minutes. Remove from muffin tins while warm. These freeze well. Makes 5 dozen.

Adolphus Fruit Tarts

Sweet Pastry
(12–18 tart shells, depending on size):

½ pound soft butter
1½ cups granulated sugar
2 eggs
4 cups all-purpose flour
½ teaspoon salt
½ teaspoon baking powder

Soften butter to room temperature, add sugar, and cream with electric mixer. Add whole eggs, one at a time, and blend well. Sift together flour, salt, and baking powder into the creamed mixture, and mix in with hands to form a ball. Wrap in clear plastic and chill in refrigerator 2 hours. This dough may be kept about 1 week refrigerated, enabling you to make only as many shells as you wish at one time. Roll out dough ¼ inch thick and cut with 2-inch round or fluted cutter. Fit into lightly greased muffin tins and bake at 375° F. for 10–12 minutes, until light golden brown. Cool pastry shells and fill with pastry cream.

Pastry Cream (2 cups)

Note: This makes a wonderful cream puff filling, too!

2 cups milk
4 egg yolks
¾ cup granulated sugar
3 tablespoons cornstarch
2 tablespoons cake flour
1 teaspoon vanilla
2 cups whipping cream (optional; doubles volume)

Scald milk. Mix egg yolks with sugar until smooth. Add cornstarch and flour and mix slowly. Add half the hot milk to egg mixture, then return all of it to the hot milk. Stir over direct low heat until it boils and thickens. Add vanilla and allow to cool. When ready to use, whip cream until stiff. Fold carefully into the cooled mixture.

Garnish cream-filled tarts with sliced bananas, raspberries, kiwi fruit, or strawberries. Then brush lightly with apricot glaze.

Apricot Glaze

5 tablespoons apricot jam
1 tablespoon water
1 teaspoon lemon juice

Bring ingredients to a boil. Cool slightly and spoon or brush over fruit. If glaze becomes too cool or too thick, add a few drops of hot water.

Here's a perennial favorite that melted the heart of many an early Texan:

Sugar Land Lemon Pie

4 eggs, separated, and whites divided
¾ cup granulated sugar
1 lemon (juice and grated rind)
baked and cooled 9-inch pie crust
2 tablespoons granulated sugar

Beat egg yolks well; blend in the ¾ cup granulated sugar and the lemon juice and grated rind. Cook in double boiler until thick. Fold in two well-beaten egg whites. Pour into pie crust. Beat the remaining 2 egg whites with 2 tablespoons granulated sugar and spread over lemon filling, being sure to seal egg white to pie crust. Bake at 350° F. for about 10 minutes, or until a golden brown.

If you've ever said in a burst of enthusiasm that you could live on pecans, you were probably right. The Indians frequently did just that according to the shipwrecked Cabeza de Vaca, who had more opportunity to study Indian customs than he ever wanted. Every two years, during the two months of a late autumn pecan harvest along the banks of the Guadalupe River, pecans were about all the Indians had to eat.

The wild but graceful pecan tree is one of those things we brag about in Texas. Our state tree, native to 152 counties, attains a height of more than 100 feet and develops a large, rounded crown. The nuts have a delicious flavor, however they are eaten—raw, toasted, plain, salted, sweetened—and they have been used to enhance the flavor of almost everything. Of course, there are substitutes, but nothing replaces pecans in pie.

Pecan Pie

3 whole eggs
3 heaping tablespoons sugar
1 tablespoon flour
1 cup white corn syrup
1 cup Texas pecans
1 teaspoon vanilla
pastry for 9-inch pie plate

Mix eggs, sugar, and flour thoroughly. Add syrup, pecans, and vanilla. Stir and pour into an unbaked pastry shell. Bake at 350° F. until brown, about 40 minutes. Cool.

The Texas pecan pie below came to *Texas Highways* from The Little House Cooking School in Victoria, where Carolyn Kamin makes the pies in the shape of Texas.

Texas Pecan Pie

Pastry (for 2 pies)

¾ cup vegetable shortening
2 cups flour, unsifted
¼–⅓ cup ice water

Filling (for 1 pie)

3 large eggs
1 cup sugar
1 stick (½ cup) unsalted butter, melted
1 cup white corn syrup
2 teaspoons vanilla
1 cup chopped pecans
¼ cup pecan halves

Preheat oven to 350° F. while making pastry. Cut shortening into flour with pastry blender or two knives until it resembles fine meal. Add water, 1 teaspoon at a time until the flour mixture holds together in a ball. Divide the dough in half, patting each flat. Freeze in individual plastic bags 15 minutes.

Filling: Break eggs into a bowl. Slowly add and stir in the sugar. Pour in melted, cooled butter. Stir in corn syrup, vanilla, and pecans.

To assemble: Remove one bag from freezer. Repeat. Roll out the dough and line either a deep glass pie plate or the Texas form pie pan. Pour half of filling in each pie and place on center oven rack for 15 minutes at 350° F., then lower oven to 325° F. and continue baking for 25 minutes. When done, the crust will appear slightly brown through the glass, or will start drawing away from the form.

Two cobblers from the feature on chuck wagon cooks Richard Bolt and John White:

Vinegar Cobbler

1¼ cups flour
½ teaspoon salt
½ cup shortening
4 tablespoons water
¼ cup apple vinegar
2 cups water
1 cup sugar
1 teaspoon vanilla
2 tablespoons margarine

Mix flour and salt and cut in shortening. Add 4 tablespoons water and mix into dough. Divide into three equal parts and roll each into a sheet ½ inch thick. Cut into strips 1 inch wide. Mix all other ingredients in small Dutch oven and heat to a boil. While boiling, drop in strips of pastry until two-thirds of it is used. Remove Dutch oven from the heat. Use the last third of the pastry to crisscross over the top. Sprinkle with 2 tablespoons margarine cut in small pieces, and bake in a 375° F. oven until the top is brown.

Sunday Cobbler

2 1-pound cans water-packed cherries (or berries), with accompanying liquid
2 cups granulated sugar (divided)
1 cup all-purpose flour (divided)
½ cup brown sugar
½ teaspoon cinnamon
½ cup butter or margarine
½ cup chopped pecans
½ cup sourdough starter (see p. 71)
2 tablespoons sugar

Pour cherries into iron Dutch oven, add 1½ cups sugar, mixed with ¼ cup flour. Mix well; cook over live coals until juice is thick and cherries are hot. Set aside. Combine the rest of the flour, sugars, and cinnamon. Cut in butter. Stir in pecans and sourdough starter. Spoon over the cherries and place the oven back on the coals. Cover with the lid and place hot coals on the lid to bake. After the top begins to brown, lift lid and with a sharp knife cut holes in the top so juice can bubble up through. When golden brown, sprinkle 2 tablespoons sugar over top crust, replace lid, and bake 1 more minute.

(On the kitchen stove, heat fruit and sugar over low heat; bake completed cobbler in oven at 425° F. for about 25 minutes.)

Bake 10 minutes at 400° F., then lower to 375° F. and continue baking for 50–60 minutes on the middle oven shelf. Crusts will be brown; an oven liner placed on the bottom oven shelf will keep both from becoming too dark.

———

And this one is from Jessie Fantroy:

Fairfield County Peach Cobbler

4 cups sliced peaches
1 cup sugar (more if peaches are tart)
½ teaspoon nutmeg or cinnamon
½ stick (4 tablespoons) butter
½ teaspoon vanilla
1 recipe pie pastry (using 2 cups flour)

Place peaches in 12-by-15-inch pan. Sprinkle sugar and nutmeg over peaches. Add butter and vanilla flavoring. Cover with pie pastry. Bake at 375° F. for 10 minutes. Reduce heat to 350° F. and cook another 30 minutes. Serves 12.

———

With all the names dropped in persimmon recipes, one of the most authoritative recipe sources is a housewife/persimmon recipe collector in Nelta, Texas, where the Virginia species grows. This is her choice:

Modena Whitlock's Persimmon Pie

1 cup persimmon pulp (see Persimmon Cake, p. 81)
2 cups sugar
1 cup milk
2 tablespoons flour
3 eggs
½ teaspoon salt
1 teaspoon nutmeg
¼ teaspoon cloves
¼ teaspoon cinnamon
9-inch pie pastry

Mix filling ingredients together and pour into unbaked pastry shell. Bake at 350° F. until the pie is set, about 1 hour.

Clarissa Nixon gathers peach blossoms. Her great-grandfather, B. L. Enderle, introduced peaches to the Hill Country.

This is one of my personal favorites, the peach pie-cobbler from June Teena Anderson, one of the Panhandle's finest cooks.

June's Peachy Pie-Cobbler

Pastry

11 tablespoons vegetable shortening
2 cups flour
pinch of salt
7 tablespoons cold water

Work shortening, flour, and salt to cornmeal consistency; then add water, 1 tablespoon at a time, tossing lightly with a fork until mixture is uniformly moist. Knead slightly. Pat and roll out as thin as possible on a floured pastry cloth.

Filling

6–8 large peaches (or 10–12 medium)
2 tablespoons fresh lemon juice
1 cup sugar
4 tablespoons flour
1 teaspoon nutmeg
¼ teaspoon cinnamon
2-crust pastry
½ stick (4 tablespoons) butter

Peel and slice peaches, then sprinkle with fresh lemon juice and set aside. Mix sugar, flour, nutmeg, and cinnamon and add to sliced peaches. *Note:* Do not add extra cinnamon unless you want peaches to darken.

Line an 8-inch square oven-proof glass dish or foil tin with crust pastry. Fill pan with peach mixture. Slice butter and place on top of peaches, then cover with top pastry. Crimp edges with fork and make slits in a flower design.

9
Other Sweets

Jack Lewis

Cookies

In the pastry kitchen, way down under Dallas' old Adolphus Hotel, creative pastry chef Jean Pierre Piaillier shared his favorite teatime recipes with me for the March 1983 issue of *Texas Highways*.

Al Rubio

Almond Tuiles

½ cup butter, melted and slightly
  browned
5 medium egg whites
1¼ cups granulated sugar
2 cups sliced almonds, with skins
1 cup flour, sifted

Preheat oven to 350° F.

For curving the cookies, prepare a
long, U-shaped mold of heavy aluminum
foil by folding over a 10-inch long sheet
of heavy foil four times lengthwise to
make a flat strip measuring 10 inches by
3 inches. Curve the long sides upward
so the strip resembles a long trough.

Stir butter over direct heat until it
becomes slightly browned. Beat egg
whites slightly with a wire whisk. Continue whisking as sugar and almonds
are added. Add flour and melted butter,
stirring to mix. Drop level teaspoonfuls
of batter onto a greased baking sheet,
flattening each cookie with the back of
a spoon. Bake only about 8 cookies at a
time, for 7–8 minutes. They will be
light brown around the edges. Remove
immediately from sheet and drop each
cookie, while still soft, briefly into the
mold. They should still be soft enough
to curve without breaking. Or simply
use a rolling pin to curve them.

Chocolate Truffles

1 pint whipping cream
½ cup granulated sugar
20 ounces semisweet chocolate,
  melted
cocoa powder for rolling
8 ounces semisweet chocolate for
  coating

Bring the cream just to a boil and add
sugar. Stir in 20 ounces of chocolate,
which has been melted over hot, not
boiling water. When chocolate has dissolved in the cream, it will be thick like
a sauce. Cool, then refrigerate covered
for 1 hour or until it is really cold.

Remove mixture from refrigerator
and stir over hot, not boiling, water until it reaches room temperature only. As
the mixture loses its chill it becomes
elastic (it should not be heated to a liquid) and can be dropped from a teaspoon in uniform walnut-size bits on a
tray covered with foil or waxed paper.
Refrigerate for 30 minutes. Roll in cocoa
powder and return to the refrigerator.

To coat: Melt remaining semisweet
chocolate over hot water. Remove
truffles from the refrigerator and dip
in melted chocolate to make a shell. Roll
in cocoa powder again. These will keep
in the refrigerator about 2 weeks.
Makes 9 dozen.

The original oatmeal cookie recipe
Texas Highways found in Oatmeal,
Texas, called for ½ cup of castor oil,
but we couldn't go through with it.
The recipe was adapted to use vege-
table oil instead.

Oatmeal Cookies

3 cups flour
¾ teaspoon baking soda
¾ teaspoon salt
¾ teaspoon ginger
⅓ cup vegetable oil
¾ cup brown sugar
1 egg
½ cup molasses
½ cup milk
1½ cups rolled oats

Lemon Icing

1 cup powdered sugar
1 tablespoon lemon juice

Sift first 4 ingredients into a large mixing bowl. Blend in oil, sugar, egg, molasses, and milk. Stir in oats. Drop by
teaspoonful onto greased baking sheet.
Bake at 350° F. for 10–12 minutes. Cool
slightly.

Combine icing ingredients. Drizzle
over cooled cookies. Makes 5 dozen.

Texas Highways presents: Texas
peanuts . . .

Peanut Butter Brownies

¾ cup peanut butter
2 cups sugar
1 cup brown sugar, firmly packed
4 eggs
1½ teaspoons vanilla extract
3 cups flour
1 tablespoon baking powder
1 teaspoon salt
½ cup Texas peanuts, chopped

Cream together peanut butter, sugar,
and brown sugar. Add eggs and vanilla
and blend well. Sift together flour, baking powder, and salt; add to creamed
mixture. Add chopped peanuts. Mix until smooth. Spread batter evenly in a
greased baking pan, 13 by 9 inches.
Bake at 350° F. for 35 minutes. Cool
slightly; add topping.

Topping

1½ cups brown sugar, firmly packed
¼ cup milk
1 tablespoon honey
1 cup peanuts, chopped

Combine first three ingredients; bring
to a boil and cook slowly 10 minutes.
Remove from heat. Add peanuts. Allow
to cool, then spread on warm brownies.
Cut into 24 squares.

. . . and Texas blueberries!

Blueberry Oatmeal Cookies

½ cup butter or margarine
1 cup firmly packed dark brown sugar
¾ cup granulated sugar
2 eggs
2¼ cups all-purpose flour
2 teaspoons baking powder
½ teaspoon salt
½ teaspoon baking soda
1½ teaspoons cinnamon
1 teaspoon vanilla
1 cup quick-cooking oats
1 cup blueberries

Preheat oven to 400° F. Cream butter
until fluffy; stir in sugars. Beat in eggs.
Add remaining ingredients except blueberries. Drop dough by heaping teaspoonfuls on greased cookie sheet.
Arrange blueberries on top of each
cookie. Bake 10–12 minutes, until
lightly browned. Cool on racks. Store
in airtight container. Makes 3 dozen.

Don't even think about making June Anderson's coconut pecan crisps unless you are prepared to eat at least two before they are cool.

June's Coconut Pecan Crisps

2 sticks (1 cup) butter
½ cup sugar
2 cups all-purpose flour
1 teaspoon vanilla
3-ounce can flaked coconut
½ cup chopped pecans
powdered sugar

Cream butter and sugar thoroughly. Add flour, vanilla flavoring, coconut, and pecans. Roll by hand into small balls. Put on an ungreased cookie sheet about an inch apart. Flatten balls with a fork which has been dipped in cold water. Bake at 350° F. for 20 minutes. Cool cookies and dust with powdered sugar. Makes 4 dozen.

M-m-macaroons

½ cup egg whites
1½ cups sugar
½ teaspoon salt
1 teaspoon vanilla
1 cup or more coconut, pecans, chopped dates, or cornflakes

Beat egg whites with electric mixer 5 minutes, until very stiff. Add sugar gradually; beat another 15 minutes. Add rest of ingredients, and drop by teaspoonfuls on greased pan. Bake about 25 minutes in 300° F. oven. Macaroons are done when you can slide one on the pan. Makes 4½ dozen.

Sugar Cakes

1 pound butter
4 cups granulated sugar
6 eggs
2 teaspoons salt
1 teaspoon nutmeg
¼ cup brandy
8 cups sifted, all-purpose flour
1 teaspoon baking powder

Cream butter and sugar. Add well-beaten eggs, salt, nutmeg, and brandy. Beat mixture well. Sift flour and baking powder together and add. Put dough in a covered bowl and refrigerate for at least 2 hours. Take from refrigerator by small pieces and roll. Slice and bake in preheated 400° F. oven 6–8 minutes or until brown. Makes 6–7 dozen cookies.

More blue-ribbon recipes from Fredericksburg's Mrs. Meta Mund:

Meta Mund's Coconut-Oatmeal Cookies

½ cup margarine
¾ cup brown sugar
¾ cup white sugar
2 medium eggs
2 cups flour
1 teaspoon baking soda
1½ cups rolled oats
1½ cups coconut
1 cup pecans
white sugar for dipping

Cream margarine, sugars, and eggs; add sifted flour and soda, then oats, coconut, and nuts. Chill overnight. Roll in small balls, dip in additional white sugar, and flatten slightly on greased and floured baking sheet. Bake in 325° F. oven 10–12 minutes. Makes 6 dozen.

Mrs. Mund's Favorite Fruit Cookies

1½ cups sugar
½ cup margarine
2 eggs
2⅔ cups sifted flour
½ teaspoon cinnamon
½ teaspoon nutmeg
½ teaspoon cloves
1 teaspoon baking soda
1 cup pecans
1 cup dates, pitted and chopped
1 cup raisins (or substitute 1 cup of candied fruit)
2 tablespoons wine (or sour milk)

Cream sugar, margarine, and eggs; add sifted dry ingredients. Add nuts, fruit, and wine. Drop by teaspoonfuls on greased and floured baking sheet. Bake at 350° F. 12–15 minutes. If you substitute shortening for the margarine, add ½ teaspoon salt with the dry ingredients. Flour on the baking sheets keeps the cookies from spreading. Makes 6 dozen.

At Fredericksburg's Pioneer Museum, members of the Gillespie County Historical Society, wearing nineteenth-century pioneer dress, host an old-fashioned Christmas celebration. The following recipe for honey cookies dates back to the founding Meusebach family. Note that no butter or other fat is necessary.

Meusebach Family Honig Plaetzchen (Honey Cookies)

1⅓ cups honey
2½ cups sugar
4½+ cups flour
4 cups pecan meats, chopped
1 tablespoon baking soda
1 teaspoon cinnamon
½ cup grape juice or whiskey
grated rind of 1 orange

Heat honey. Add all other ingredients. Use enough flour to make a stiff dough and shape into rolls for icebox cookies. Cover and refrigerate overnight. Slice thin and bake on greased sheet in 325° F. oven 10–15 minutes. Makes 6 dozen.

From the Maxey House at Paris:

Long Family Rock Cookies

1 cup sugar
⅔ cup butter, softened
2 eggs, beaten
2½ cups flour
½ teaspoon cinnamon
½ teaspoon nutmeg
½ teaspoon baking soda, dissolved in 1 tablespoon hot water
1 pound raisins
1 pound pecans, chopped
powdered sugar

Cream sugar and butter; add eggs. Add flour, spices, and dissolved baking soda. Mix well; add raisins and pecans.

Drop by teaspoonfuls onto greased cookie sheet. Bake at 375° F. for 15 minutes. When cool, roll in powdered sugar. Allow to harden in an airtight container for at least 3 days before serving. Makes 6 dozen.

Nuts and Candies

The Texas Department of Agriculture offers suggestions for dressing up glorious Texas pecans for gifts. Shell the pecans, or buy them shelled, and prepare two types to present in twin snack jars: salted, piquant nuts and orange-flavored ones with spice and sugar.

©Don Heit

Ideal Christmas gifts: pralines and divinity crunchy with Texas pecans; or pecans simply sugared and spiced

Salted Pecans

Bake a single layer of pecans on a baking sheet at 300° F. until brown. Watch them; shake the pan if necessary. Remove and pour on 1 tablespoon melted butter per cup of pecans. Salt, stir well, and add ⅛ teaspoon of cayenne pepper (optional). Drain pecans on plain paper before storing.

Spicy Orange Pecans

1½ cups powdered sugar
2 tablespoons cornstarch
1 teaspoon cinnamon
¼ teaspoon allspice
⅛ teaspoon salt
2 tablespoons orange peel, freshly grated (or cheat)
2 egg whites, slightly beaten
3 tablespoons freshly squeezed orange juice (or cheat)
2 cups pecans

Sift together sugar, cornstarch, spices, and salt; stir in orange peel. Blend egg whites with orange juice; stir in pecans, coating each piece completely. Drain thoroughly. Then roll in sugar mixture to coat well. Spread on cookie sheet; do not allow pecans to touch. Bake at 250° F. for 20–25 minutes or until dry. Cool before storing in covered container.

Yet another treatment for Christmas pecans leaves a thin, sweet coating. Pair these spiced pecans with Annette Gragg's roasted, vinegary pecans, below.

Spiced Pecans

1 cup sugar
1 teaspoon cinnamon
⅓ cup evaporated milk
1 teaspoon vanilla
1½ cups nuts

Cook sugar, cinnamon, and milk until mixture forms a soft ball in water. Add vanilla and mix with nuts to coat. Pour onto waxed paper and separate as soon as nuts are cool enough.

Annette Gragg's Roasted Pecans

2½–3 quarts shelled pecans
1 tablespoon vinegar
2 dashes Worcestershire sauce
3 tablespoons butter or margarine, melted
seasoning salt

Mix ingredients until nuts are thoroughly coated. Spread on cookie sheet and bake in 200° F. oven for 2 hours. Stir occasionally while cooking. Sprinkle with seasoning salt to taste. When cool, keep them in the freezer in jars for special occasions.

Texas pecans make such good candy; it's no coincidence that our favorite candy recipes for Christmas giving usually have pecans. We offered two of the most popular recipes for Divinity.

Patsy Goforth's Divinity

2½ cups sugar
½ cup light corn syrup
¼ teaspoon salt
½ cup water
2 extra large egg whites
1 teaspoon vanilla
1 cup chopped, toasted pecans or candied fruit

Cook sugar, corn syrup, salt, and water in heavy saucepan with candy thermometer clipped to the side of the pan. Stir until the sugar is dissolved; then cook without stirring to 260° F. (a few drops form a hard ball when dropped into cold water and removed). Remove from heat. Beat egg whites at high speed on mixer to stiff peaks, then pour syrup in a fine stream over egg whites as beater turns. Beat 4–5 minutes until candy holds its shape when beaters are lifted (falling mixture mounds upon itself). Add vanilla and nuts with a wooden spoon. Drop quickly by teaspoonfuls on waxed paper. Makes about 3 dozen pieces.

When Mary Faulk Koock gave us Christmas at Green Pastures, she also gave us:

Texana's Wonderful Divinity

2 cups sugar
½ cup white corn syrup
½ cup water
⅛ teaspoon salt
2 egg whites
1 teaspoon vanilla
1½ cups chopped pecans

Place sugar, corn syrup, water, and salt in a heavy saucepan over low heat. Cook slowly, scraping sides of pan with a rubber spatula occasionally. Cook until a soft ball forms when dropped in cold water, one that can be picked up and rolled between finger and thumb (240° F. on a candy thermometer).

Have egg whites beaten stiff. With beater on medium speed, slowly pour one-third of the syrup over the egg whites, continuing to beat.

Return remaining syrup to heat and cook to a hard ball (265° F.). While still beating egg white mixture, add syrup. Continue beating approximately 6–10 minutes, until candy begins to lose gloss. Add vanilla; then stir in pecans.

Have waxed paper over newspaper or heavy brown paper ready on kitchen counter. With two iced tea spoons, quickly form and drop the candy. Work quickly; have someone help if possible.

Never-Fail Peanut Brittle

3 cups sugar
1⅓ cups white corn syrup
½ cup water
4 cups raw peanuts
1 tablespoon butter
1 teaspoon vanilla
2½ teaspoons soda

Mix sugar, corn syrup, and water in a 3-quart saucepan. Boil until thread spins or until temperature has reached 234° F. Add peanuts. Stir constantly until temperature reaches 300° F. Remove from heat and quickly stir in butter, vanilla, and soda. Mix well and pour mixture onto 2 buttered cookie sheets. Spread as thin as possible with spoon. Let brittle cool thoroughly. Turn brittle over and break into bite-size pieces. Store peanut brittle in airtight container in cool, dry place until ready to serve. Makes about 3 pounds.

Texans have more praline recipes than you can shake a pecan-wood stick at. Here are some of the best for *Texas Highways* readers, from three good cooks. The chewy variety, as made by Josephine Sims of Boerne, is the hardest to find:

Jo Sims' Chewy Pralines

1 cup sugar
1 cup light corn syrup
pinch salt
¼ cup margarine
⅞ cup milk
2 cups pecans, whole or broken
½ teaspoon vanilla

Cook sugar, syrup, and salt rapidly to firm ball stage (250° F.), stirring occasionally. Gradually add margarine, milk, and nuts, so that the mixture continues to boil. Cook over medium heat to firm ball stage, about 25 minutes, stirring constantly to keep mixture from sticking. Add vanilla and allow to stand until mixture stops bubbling. Drop spoonfuls onto well-buttered baking sheet or platter. Cool at room temperature. Place in refrigerator to harden. To remove from pan, place pan on a moist, hot towel. Wrap each piece in wax paper. Makes about 30 pralines.

Historian Larry Hodge is a frequent contributor to *Texas Highways*.

Larry Hodge's Larrupin' Pralines

2½ cups sugar, divided
⅔ cup evaporated milk
2 cups pecans
1 teaspoon vanilla extract
1 tablespoon butter or margarine

Caramelize ½ cup sugar. Meanwhile, cook 2 cups sugar and milk in saucepan. Add caramelized sugar and pecans. Cook to soft ball stage (236° F.). Remove from heat. Add vanilla and butter, but do not stir. When cooler, beat with wooden spoon until mixture just begins to hold its shape. Drop spoonfuls quickly onto waxed paper backed with several layers of newspaper. Makes about 40.

This one, published December 1982 in *Texas Highways*, had its origin in Galveston with the late Io Briggs. Now her son-in-law, L. G. Meier, and daughter, Babe, make the recipe each year.

The L. G. Meiers' Pecan Pralines

2 cups light brown sugar
1 cup white sugar
¾ cup milk
dash salt
2 cups broken pecans
1 tablespoon margarine
½ teaspoon vanilla

Put sugars, milk, and salt into saucepan; bring to boil and boil for 5 minutes, stirring constantly. Add pecans; stir and boil for 5 more minutes. Remove from heat; add margarine and vanilla, and stir for 2 minutes. Either pour into paper baking cups or drop 2 tablespoons for each praline onto a greased pan. If paper baking cups are used, remove while pralines are still warm.

When cookies won't satisfy those apparently insatiable cravings for chocolate and nuts, try Porteño Chocolate Chunks. As a bride, I invented this recipe before its time, when a thorough search of Buenos Aires, Argentina, produced neither chocolate chips nor pecans. Now, the idea's time has come.

Porteño Chocolate Chunks

12 ounces semisweet cooking chocolate
1¼ cups flour, sifted before measuring
½ teaspoon salt
½ teaspoon soda
½ cup butter
⅓ cup white sugar
⅓ cup brown sugar, firmly packed
1 large egg, beaten
1 teaspoon vanilla
1 cup chopped walnuts (or pecans)
powdered sugar

Preheat oven to 375° F. On a chopping board, chop cooking chocolate into gravel-sized nuggets. Use the slivers and chocolate dust, too. Sift flour, measure, and resift with salt and soda. Cream butter until smooth; add sugars and beat until fluffy. Add egg and vanilla and beat until light. Mix in dry ingredients; then fold in nuts and chocolate. Drop by teaspoonfuls in rows of four onto greased baking sheet, allowing them room to spread. Bake 8 minutes. Remove while soft, and roll in powdered sugar. Makes 7 dozen.

Whenever you have leftover egg whites, make my favorite meringue kisses. One is never enough, so I call them

Kiss-Me-Agains

3 egg whites
1 cup sugar
1 teaspoon vinegar
1 teaspoon vanilla
1 cup chopped pecans or chocolate chips, or ½ cup of each

Preheat oven to 250° F. Line baking sheets with plain, unglazed paper. Beat egg whites to a froth, starting slowly and increasing to high speed. Beat until stiff, but not dry. Then add sugar, 2 tablespoons at a time, beating constantly until completely dissolved. Beat in vinegar and vanilla until they disappear. Fold in pecans and/or chocolate chips. Drop from teaspoons onto baking sheets about 1 inch apart. Bake for 20 minutes. Allow to stand for 5 minutes before lifting from paper with a spatula. Makes about 3 dozen.

Variation: When cool, carefully stick the flat side of 2 kisses together with orange cream filling:

2 tablespoons butter
⅓ cup powdered sugar
1 teaspoon orange juice
1 teaspoon freshly grated orange peel

Note: If you make these when you're home alone, nobody has to know how many you made. That can be our little secret.

10

Christmas

Jack Lewis

What to Serve

At Christmas *Texas Highways* frequently addresses the issue of ethnic traditions of the rich Texan heritage. So many of our customs have been adapted from the German and English that we think of them as our own. Others are very colorful: the Posadas from Mexico; the Lucia Bride from Sweden; the Czech apple strudel twist. Perhaps some of these will spark an idea from your own ancestry.

Bob Parvin

Julie Leavens of Houston enacts the Swedish tradition of the Lucia Bride at Christmas time. She wears a white dress and a crown of white candles when she serves Lucia Buns to her family.

Traditional Eggnog

2 eggs, separated
2 tablespoons sugar
2 ounces bourbon
½ pint whipping cream, whipped
ground nutmeg

Beat egg yolks until thick. Add sugar and bourbon. Fold in cream and then stiffly beaten egg whites. Serve eggnog very cold with a sprinkle of freshly ground nutmeg. Serves four.

If the party occasion dictates the traditional hot punch, try this one from the restored Brent House at Old City Park in Dallas. The beverage is served, along with hot apple mincemeat cobbler and rum cake, as an alternative to hot chocolate or coffee during the annual Christmas Candlelight Tour.

Holiday Wassail

2–3 quarts sweet apple cider
3 cups orange juice (or a 6-ounce can frozen, mixed with 18 ounces water)
1 cup fresh lemon juice
1 cup pineapple juice
1 stick cinnamon
whole cloves
raw honey to taste

Mix all ingredients, and simmer together 2 minutes. Serve hot. (Rum may be served on the side.)

Another wassail recipe, this one from Jessie Fantroy:

Mrs. Fantroy's Hot Wassail

3 oranges
3 lemons
1 ounce cinnamon sticks
1 tablespoon allspice
1½ cups water
1½ cups sugar
1 gallon sweet apple cider

Squeeze the juice from the oranges and lemons and reserve. Place rinds and spices in a saucepan. Add the water, cover, and simmer 2½ hours. Strain the liquid and pour over the sugar. Add the fruit juices and apple cider. Heat almost to boiling, but do not boil. Serve very hot.

Czech legend maintains that a child who can make it through Christmas Eve without tasting a single morsel before the big evening feast will see a golden pig dancing on the ceiling. No one ever has been able to resist the apple strudel or the braided sweet bread, much less the quick-snitch pastries and anise-flavored cookies. The typical fare in Texas, according to Alice Prasatik of Austin, includes red snapper, trout, or catfish, substituted for the Czechs' specially-bred Trebon carp. Side dishes might include crisp, fried cauliflower florets, carrots, and a steamed cabbage salad. The menu always includes creamed potatoes or potato salad with mayonnaise. A bowl of fresh fruit symbolizes the holiday season.

Alice Prasatik's Apple Strudel (Jablkovy Zavin)

Dough (for 3 strudel)

3½ cups flour
¼ cup sugar
¼ teaspoon salt
1 cup lukewarm water
2 tablespoons butter, melted
1 egg

Sift flour, sugar, and salt; place in large bowl. Make a well; add water, warm melted butter, and egg. Mix until flour is blended. Place dough on well-floured board and knead until flexible and sticky. Divide into three portions. Place two in separate well-greased bowls, grease top, cover with waxed paper, and seal with tight lid. Refrigerate or freeze to use later. Place third portion in greased bowl; grease top. Cover; set bowl in hot water. While dough is resting, make filling.

Filling (for 1 strudel)

8–10 large apples
1–2 teaspoons cinnamon
¾ cup chopped pecans or walnuts
2 slices toast rolled into fine crumbs
12 vanilla wafers rolled into fine crumbs
1–1½ cups sugar
1 ounce white seedless raisins
½ cup coconut (optional)
¼ pound minus 2 tablespoons butter, melted

Peel apples; slice thin. Mix rest of ingredients except butter. Roll warm dough on a floured bread board, rolling from center into a square. Flop it onto a large, well-floured cloth on a table and start stretching the dough by placing hands under it, palms up, and pulling from center with finger tips. Then stretch ends until dough is paper thin. Brush with melted butter. Spread half of crumb mixture, then add apple slices. Add remaining crumb mixture and remaining butter. Starting at one side, roll the pastry one turn, and tighten it. Then lift the cloth and gradually roll the pastry like a jelly roll. Seal ends, brush off excess flour, and place carefully on a greased cookie sheet, in a crescent shape. Butter strudel, sprinkle cinnamon and sugar on top, or glaze with beaten egg yolk. Bake at 375° F. 45 minutes and at 325° F. 15 minutes, until lightly browned. Serve warm, sliced.

Seven sisters in Geronimo, Texas, annually recreate an early Texas scene, an orphanage begun by a Lutheran minister, Louis C. Ervendberg, to house nineteen orphaned immigrant children. The Timmermann sisters, descendants of the Ervendberg family, have lived all their lives in the two-story farmhouse in Geronimo. At Christmas, they spend 5 days assembling decorations for a 10-foot tree, hanging antique ornaments and cookies on the tree, and reproducing a scene of the old Ervendberg homestead and orphanage. Each year, the sisters create a new cookie design to increase the variety of cookies on the tree.

Christmas Tree Cookies

1 pound granulated sugar
½ pound butter (2 sticks)
3 eggs
1 teaspoon vanilla
1 pound flour (3½–4 cups)
1 teaspoon cinnamon (or to taste)
grated rind of ½ lemon

Preheat oven to 350° F. Cream sugar and butter until light. Add eggs, beating well after each addition. Add vanilla. Stir in flour and cinnamon. Blend in lemon rind. Divide dough into two portions, wrap in waxed paper, and chill 1–2 hours. Roll each portion separately on a floured surface to a scant ¼ inch thick. Cut with Christmas cookie cutters. Use a wooden pick or skewer point to make a hole if you plan to hang the cookies on the tree. Bake on greased cookie sheet at 350° F. for 12–15 minutes. Cool on rack and decorate. Makes about 3½ dozen.

For another version of the Timmermann Sisters' Christmas Tree Cookies, use sifted powdered sugar instead of granulated sugar and leave out the cinnamon and lemon rind. Brush cooled cookies with 1 slightly beaten egg white. Decorate with assorted colored sugar crystals, chocolate shot, red and green candied cherries, and gold and silver dragees. To hang on tree, attach ornament hooks.

For some reason best known to early missionaries, a Sicilian martyr, Santa Lucia, became the Swedish symbol of light. The lady lost her eyes, it seems, when a pagan suitor lost his heart to them, supposedly at the darkest time of the year. Hence, Santa Lucia, called Lucia Bride in Sweden, is honored with many lights.

Her feast day, December 13, marks the beginning of the holiday season. The oldest daughter in a Swedish home enacts the role of Lucia Bride. She wears a white dress and crimson sash; on her head, she wears a lingon-leaf crown adorned with lighted white candles. She wakens each member of the family, leaving coffee and buns at the bedside. In a small village, one

John Suhrstedt

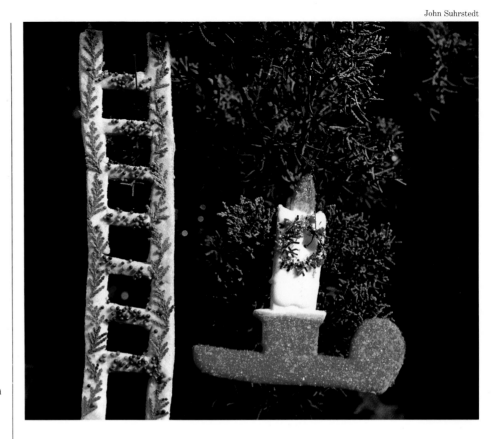

girl may be elected to visit every household; in a city, there may be many Lucias, with one chosen to visit hospitals and nursing homes.

The following recipe of Lucia buns, from Ida Kjellberg of Houston, is used when the Linneas of Texas Society commemorates Saint Lucy's Day, or Luciadagen, on the Sunday nearest the actual date. Lucia buns, by the way, should be X-shaped, for the Greek letter *chi*, the first letter in the name Christ.

Ida Kjellberg's Lucia Buns

1 cup milk
¼–½ teaspoon cardamon seed, crushed
¾ cup sugar
1 teaspoon salt
½ cup soft butter
2 packages active dry yeast
¾ cup warm water (105–115° F.)
6½ cups sifted flour
2 eggs
½ cup ground blanched almonds
raisins
1 egg yolk
1 tablespoon water

Heat milk until it bubbles around edge of pan. Remove from heat; add cardamom, sugar, salt, butter; stir until butter is melted. Let cool to lukewarm. Sprinkle yeast over warm water in a big bowl; stir until dissolved. Add milk mixture. Add 3½ cups flour; beat with wooden spoon until smooth. Beat in eggs and almonds, then the remaining flour. Mix the last by hand until it forms a soft dough, leaving the sides of the bowl.

Turn dough onto lightly floured pastry cloth; cover with bowl. Let rise 10 minutes. Turn the dough over to coat with flour; knead until smooth, about 5 minutes. Place in lightly greased bowl; turn to bring up greased side. Cover with towel; let rise in a warm place until double in bulk, about 1½ hours. Punch down; turn out onto floured cloth.

Divide and shape: With palms, roll pencil-thin strips and cut into 5-inch lengths. On greased cookie sheet, cross two strips to make an X and curl each end into a small coil. Place a raisin in the center of each coil. Cover; let rise in warm place until double in bulk, 40 minutes. Preheat oven to 400° F. Brush buns with egg yolk mixed with 1 tablespoon water. Bake 12–15 minutes or until golden brown.

Gifts from the Kitchen

In December 1982, recipes for some of my favorite kitchen gifts were published in *Texas Highways*, along with suggestions for adding a bit of Texana to the wrap.

Rather than gift-wrap a candy dish, for example, fill it with homemade Texas pecan candy, and tie it with a pretty ribbon. Or buy your favorite Yankee the Texas-shaped cake or cornbread pan. Use it, first, to make Longneck Cake. Then wrap the cake in clear plastic and return it to the pan. For the presentation, tie a red bandana around the Panhandle. This cake, made with beer, chopped dates, and toasted pecans, will be popular with those who admit openly that they don't like fruitcake.

© Don Heit

Thoughtful gift for a cook: Longneck Cake in a Texas-shaped baking pan

Longneck Cake

Note: This recipe fits an 8-inch square pan, or it can be doubled and baked in a 10-inch tube pan. To bake it in a Texas-shaped cake or cornbread pan, remove ⅔ cup batter before baking; bake that later in a small mold for a sample. For a tube pan, increase cooking time to 1 hour and 10 minutes.

½ cup shortening
1 cup dark brown sugar, packed
1 extra large egg
1 cup chopped dates
½ cup chopped nuts (toasted dry)
1½ cups sifted flour
1 teaspoon baking soda
¼ teaspoon salt
½ teaspoon cinnamon
¼ teaspoon allspice
¼ teaspoon cloves
1 cup beer (let foam settle before measuring)

Preheat oven to 350° F. Butter and flour the baking pan. Cream shortening with brown sugar, add egg, and mix until fluffy. Stir in dates and nuts. Sift dry ingredients together and work into the date-nut mixture (it will be stiff). Gradually stir in beer, mixing well with a wooden spoon. Bake 45 minutes or until a toothpick inserted in the top comes out clean. Cool in pan on wire rack for 20 minutes. Remove cake from pan and cool right side up. Sprinkle with powdered sugar.

If you like to start your Christmas baking 6 weeks ahead, KVIL Dallas News Director Andy McCollum offers an old family recipe for Thieves' Fruitcake. It's easy enough to make, he says, but hanging onto it for 6 weeks may be difficult.

"The cake is called Thieves' Fruitcake because it really is so good that people steal it," says McCollum. "We took one along on an outing on Lake Travis once. While we were out in the boat fishing, someone broke into the cabin and stole *only* the fruitcake. Hence the name!"

Ideally, the cake should be aged 6 weeks in the refrigerator, wrapped in a bourbon-soaked cheesecloth and sealed in a cake tin. Every week, the cake should be unwrapped, sprinkled with bourbon whiskey, wrapped again, and resealed for cold storage. The last time, the cake can be cut and the pieces individually wrapped and sealed or tied with a colorful ribbon. Collected into a decorated basket, the pieces could be an office party take-home treat.

Part of the tradition, which dates back two generations, is a silver ring baked into the cake for good luck.

Thieves' Fruitcake

2 cups whole candied cherries
2 cups white seedless raisins
2 cups bourbon
2 cups softened butter
2 cups dark brown sugar, packed
2 cups white sugar
8 eggs, separated
5 cups sifted all-purpose flour
4 cups pecan halves
1½ teaspoons baking powder
1 teaspoon salt
1 teaspoon nutmeg

Combine fruit and bourbon in a covered bowl in the refrigerator overnight. Drain and reserve the liquor. Beat the butter till fluffy, add sugars gradually, then egg yolks. Combine ½ cup flour with the pecans. Sift remaining flour with baking powder, salt, and nutmeg. Add 2 cups of flour mixture to creamed mixture and beat thoroughly. Add reserved liquor and rest of flour mixture alternately, beginning and ending with flour. Beat egg whites till stiff, but not dry. Fold into mixture. Add fruits and pecans and blend. Fill a 10-inch tube cake pan, lined with wax paper, to one inch from the top. Put the rest of the batter in a similarly lined loaf pan.

"Insert one silver ring in the batter with your finger," says McCollum. "Lick batter off finger, then place cakes in oven."

Bake tube cake at 275° F. 4½–5 hours. Bake loaf cake at the same temperature 2–3 hours. Cool 3 hours. Wrap cakes in bourbon-soaked cheesecloth and store, refrigerated, in a cake tin for at least 2 weeks. Keep "boozey-wet" by unwrapping and sprinkling the cakes once a week.

The cake can be presented whole after aging 2 weeks. Pack the cake as described above, and send along a bottle of good bourbon and proper instructions on what to do with it. Be sure to mention that whoever gets the silver ring, according to the legend, will have good luck all year.

For a different twist to the traditional fruitcake gift, a pretty jar of Dallasite Margaret Allison's fruitcake sauce combines well with a plain gingerbread layer. Either make the gingerbread or include a box of gingerbread mix in the gift. For presentation, leave the pecans out of the sauce and package them separately. Include instructions for assembling the dessert.

Fruitcake Sauce

½ cup candied pineapple
½ cup candied cherries
1 cup raisins
2 cups brown sugar
½ cup coffee cream
2 tablespoons flour
pinch salt
1 cup pecans (packaged separately)

Heat everything except pecans to boiling and boil 2–3 minutes. Reheat to serve over warm gingerbread, adding pecans at the last.

El Stack-Pack, a gift with a Tex-Mex accent, is the result of a combination of ideas from the three Johns sisters who grew up in Boerne, Texas: Carolyn Scrafford, Betsy Simpson, and Josephine Sims. Collect the gift items, except candy, in a basket; tuck the candy inside a piñata. Present the two together. Choose from some of the gift items suggested in December 1982: leche quemada candy and polvorones cookies, a chili-cheese log, a jar of jalapeño jelly, chili seasoning packages (however many alarms you think the recipient can handle), nacho chips, peppers, and sauces.

© Hiram Parent

Mexican Gold Poppy finds a home in El Paso's Franklin Mountains.

Leche Quemada

2 quarts milk
1 pound granulated sugar
pecan halves

Boil milk with sugar, stirring occasionally, about 2 hours, until you can pull mixture away from the sides of the pan with a spoon (it will move back). Pour into a greased square pan and, when cool, cut into squares. Press a pecan half into each square.

Carolyn's Polvorones (Mexican Sugar Cookies)

2 cups sifted flour
¾ cup sugar
½ teaspoon cinnamon
1 cup soft butter

Sift together flour, cinnamon, and sugar. Cream butter with mixer, and gradually add flour mixture. Pinch off small pieces of dough. Shape into 24 patties and put on an ungreased cookie sheet. Bake at 300° F. for 25 minutes. Sift extra sugar and cinnamon over the cookies when you remove them from the oven.

When *Texas Highways* sent Bob Parvin to sample the *pastitso* and *spanakopita* at the Dallas Greek Food Festival at the Holy Trinity Greek Orthodox Church in 1980, Bob found a lot of food for thought as well. Standing on the strong faith and traditions of one of the oldest centers of civilization, Greek refugees could survive the most difficult circumstances and rise to the peak of success.

"The will to remain independent is strong among Greeks, even today. . . . Next to the family, the church and its community are the binding factors in Greek life by ancient tradition. Beyond that, it's every man for himself."

Those on the gift list of Plato Karayanis, Dallas Opera general director, and his wife, Dorothy, fare especially well at Christmas. The Karayanises give either a Northern European–type stollen for Christmas breakfast or, drawing on their Greek heritage, a tin of baklava or Basilopita (St. Basil's bread), to be cut on New Year's Eve.

Karayanis says the Basilopita, in which a lucky coin is always baked, conjures sweet memories of the aroma of bread baking in his late mother's kitchen. "According to the Greek tradition, the father or grandfather broke off one piece at a time of the New Year's loaf and passed it around in memory of St. Basil," he says.

Basilopita

½ cup spice water (instructions follow)
3 envelopes dry yeast
9–10 cups all-purpose flour
2 cups sugar
1½ cups milk
2 teaspoons salt
½ pound butter, softened
½ teaspoon pulverized mastika (available at import stores)
6 eggs (save 1 for glazing top)
sesame seeds, slivered almonds, or cloves for garnish
3 dimes, sterilized by boiling

To make spice water, boil 1 stick cinnamon and 6 cloves in 1 cup water until reduced by half, then strain.

Dissolve yeast in lukewarm spice water (105–115° F.), adding 1 cup flour and 1 tablespoon sugar. Allow to rise till it becomes spongy, about 20 minutes.

Scald milk in separate pan, then cool to lukewarm. Add to the milk the remaining sugar, salt, butter, and mastika granules that have been pulverized with a mortar and pestle. Beat 5 eggs and add to milk mixture. Combine with yeast mixture; then mix in remaining flour, stirring with a wooden spoon until manageable. Knead well 10–15 minutes on a floured board. Let rise until doubled in bulk (about 1 hour) and punch down. Repeat. Divide dough into three parts, slipping a dime into each.

Randy Green

Form dough into three flat, round 8-inch pita-type loaves, spreading them on buttered cookie sheets or pie pans. Brush tops with slightly beaten egg. Sprinkle each loaf with sesame seeds or outline the numerals of the New Year's date with almonds or cloves and fill in the numbers with sesame seeds. Allow dough to rise till double in size and bake at 350° F. about 40 minutes, or until golden brown. Makes three 8-inch loaves.

Nobody can say for sure when the first Italian drifted into Texas, but according to legend, Amerigo Vespucci, for whom our continent was named, may have sighted the Texas coast in 1497. Wherever immigrants settled, they brought Old World culture to farming and the sale of produce. Religious and family-oriented, they also brought appreciation for art and music.

Italian cuisine is a common denominator for everybody; the recipes lend themselves to every occasion. March 19 is St. Joseph's Day, observed with feasting by Italians. *Texas Highways* visited a St. Joseph's Table with Jennifer Holder Gordon:

"The meal is comparable to the feasts of the Olympian gods, a sight to behold and a pleasure to gobble. The altar is only one small part of the production . . ."

While men stir life into millions of wiggling spaghetti strands in cauldrons of boiling water outside, women hover over hot stoves in little kitchens overseeing bubbling spaghetti sauce and simmering vegetables, from artichokes to zucchini. A giant fish, with head intact and mouth gaping, is garnished with fruits and vegetables for the centerpiece.

We all have our favorite Italian, or almost Italian, recipes. *Struffoli* makes a nice holiday treat; cold antipasto is delightful with salad and crackers.

Recipes with an Italian flavor make nice holiday gifts. Thoughtful cook Gail Griffin's antipasto holds special appeal for those who are diet conscious. Gail presents this as part of an hors d'oeuvre package, but it is especially good when mixed into salads.

Gail Griffin's Antipasto

4 ounces processed Swiss cheese
2 ounces hard salami
10-ounce jar Heinz spiced onions
4½-ounce can mushrooms
2 7-ounce jars stuffed green olives
2 6-ounce cans ripe olives
2-ounce jar chopped pimientos
2 12-ounce jars Trappey's Dulcito salad peppers
juice of peppers and equal amount of salad oil
3 medium carrots, blanched in boiling water
4 large ribs celery, blanched in boiling water
¼ head raw cauliflower
1–3 2-ounce cans chopped anchovies (optional)

Slice or cube all ingredients into small pieces. Mix in a large bowl, cover, and let stand in refrigerator for several days, stirring occasionally. Seal in sterilized jars. Turn each jar over from time to time. Makes 6–7 pints.

Another Italian-flavored treat good for holiday giving comes from model Helen Martin Brockie, who claims a strong legacy of traditions from her family. Struffoli, she says, is "a sort of teacake made only at Christmas and shaped into a wreath." For Helen, the tradition dates back to childhood in Chicago, where she and her sister used to help their mother and aunt make the sweet.

Struffoli

3 whole eggs
½ teaspoon vanilla
¼ teaspoon salt

2½ cups flour, or more
hot oil for frying
1 cup honey
1 tablespoon sugar
confetti candies or colored sugar
cherries and holly leaves for decoration

Beat eggs, add vanilla and salt, and stir in enough flour to make a soft, firm dough. Roll out pastry and cut in strips ½ inch wide. Roll each strip in your hands into the shape of a pencil. Cut the strips in small pieces, rolling each into a ball the size of a small marble, no bigger than ½ inch in diameter. Deep-fry pastry bits a few at a time in 2 inches of hot oil until golden, 3–4 minutes only. Do not brown. Place on paper towels to drain. Heat honey with sugar, and coat each ball with the mixture. Turn all out on an 8-inch plate and form a ring about 4 inches high and 3 inches thick. Sprinkle with tiny confetti candies or red and green sugar. Decorate with holly leaves and cherries around the edge. Cool in refrigerator. Remove when hardened and allow to warm to room temperature. Cut like a cake and serve with a sweet liqueur or espresso.

Gifts related to hobbies say a lot about the giver who shares something he or she holds dear (or deer, if the giver is a hunter). Dallas investment banker Bob Peterson makes venison pâté for close friends:

Venison Pâté

1 pound sliced bacon
2 tablespoons butter
2 onions, chopped
2 pounds ground pork (half fat, half lean)
1 pound ground venison
1 pound chicken livers, finely chopped
3 cloves garlic, crushed
½ teaspoon ground allspice
¼ teaspoon ground cloves
¼ teaspoon ground nutmeg
3 eggs, beaten to mix
1 cup heavy cream

¼ cup brandy
salt
freshly ground black pepper
1 cup shelled pistachios (optional)
2 slices cooked ham ¼ inch thick (about ¾ pound) cut in strips
2 bay leaves

Luting Paste

½ cup flour
4–5 tablespoons water

This quantity can be halved, or doubled to bake in 2 terrines. If possible, the terrine should have an airhole so the mixture can be tested with a skewer without removing the lid.

Method: Line with bacon a 4-quart terrine or casserole that has a tight-fitting cover. Reserve a few slices for the top. Melt the butter in a skillet and sauté the onion until soft but not brown. Mix the onion with the pork, venison, chicken livers, garlic, allspice, cloves, nutmeg, eggs, cream, brandy, and plenty of salt and pepper. (The mixture should taste very spicy, but do not swallow any because it contains raw pork.) Stir in the pistachios, if used. Spread a third of the mixture in the lined terrine, add a layer of half the ham strips; top with another third of the pork mixture and the rest of the ham strips. Add last third of pork mixture and then put the remaining bacon slices on top, trimming the edge, if necessary. Place the bay leaves on top of the bacon and cover. Heat the oven to 350° F. while you make the luting paste.

For the luting paste: Mix the flour with the water to a soft paste. Do not overmix or the paste will become elastic. Seal the gap around the terrine lid with paste and set the terrine in a roasting pan half filled with hot water (a water bath). Bring to a boil on top of the stove, then transfer to the oven and cook for 1¾–2 hours or until a skewer or wire inserted through the hole in the lid into the center of the terrine mixture for ½ minute is hot to the touch when withdrawn. (If the lid has no hole, lift it to test the terrine.)

Leave the terrine covered until cool. Remove the lid, set a plate with a 2-pound weight on top of the pâté, and chill for several hours or overnight. Remove the weight and replace the lid. The terrine is best kept for 3–4 days or up to a week so the flavor matures. Serve with cornichons.

11

Something Else

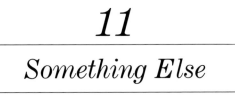

John Suhrstedt

An unusual jelly is made from the fruit (*tuna*) of the prickly pear cactus. This recipe is from *Texas Highways'* May 1982 feature on the prickly pear.

Cactus Jelly

1 gallon cactus *tunas*, gathered carefully (see p. 40)
water, enough to show through the fruit

Prepare the fruit, peel, and cut into quarters. Place in a saucepan, seeds and all, with water. Bring to a gentle boil, cover, and allow the fruit to cook for about an hour. Strain the juice from the pulp and seeds.

3¾ cups cactus fruit juice
½ cup lemon juice
1½ boxes fruit pectin (Sure-Jell)
6 cups sugar

Add lemon juice and fruit pectin to the strained juice. Bring mixture to a boil and add sugar. Allow the mixture to cook for 3 minutes.

Remove the jelly from heat and allow to cool for 45 minutes. Skim off foam and pour the jelly into hot, sterilized jars. Seal the jars immediately with canning lids or allow the jelly to set and seal it with melted paraffin.

Alternative recipe, from Betsy Simpson of San Antonio:

Betsy's Cactus Jelly

2¾ cups cactus juice
½ cup lemon juice, strained
7 cups sugar
6-ounce bottle Certo fruit pectin

Juice: After gathering and preparing 4 quarts of fruit, wash fruit in a colander, cut each pear in half, and remove the blossom end. Place the fruit in an 8-quart pan and add 1 cup water. Cook for 20 minutes, then put through a food press and strain juice through cheesecloth. At this point, juice may be frozen until ready for use.

Put cactus juice, lemon juice, and sugar in the 8-quart pan. Mix and place

Jack Lewis

over high heat. Bring to a boil, stirring constantly, then stir in Certo at once and boil hard for 1 minute, continuing to stir. Remove from heat and skim off foam with a metal spoon. Pour into hot, sterilized jars and seal with lids or cover with hot paraffin. Let stand overnight to set.

If you ask five people what to do with the wild elderberry growing along your fence, you may get five different answers, advising you to use it for food, drink, medicine, whistles, or shrubs—and some of those uses will have multiple applications. Elderberry fans range from European artisans to Indian chiefs. The plant itself is a subject of Old World folklore.

In 1985, when writer Howard Peacock explored the various uses, *Texas Highways* dubbed the botanical *Sambucus* "The Incredible Edible Elderberry." Peacock borrowed an elderberry pie recipe from naturalist Bradford Angier and witnessed the cooking of elderberry blossom fritters in the kitchen of Carmine Stahl, executive director of the Houston Audubon Society.

Certainly, Stahl's Elder-Blow Wine changed Peacock's perspective on the *Arsenic and Old Lace* plot, wherein two little old ladies laced the beverage with poison to commit murder. Peacock pointed out, too, that Dr. Alfred Kinsey occasionally put aside his research statistics on sex to concentrate on making chutney and a dessert variation called Elderberry Rob.

If you have a bush with elderberries, you'll probably think of something else.

Papa Stahl's Elder Flower Fritters

2 cups unblemished elder flowers
1 cup flour
1 tablespoon sugar
1 teaspoon baking powder
2 eggs
½ cup milk
cooking oil, at least 1 inch deep in frying pan
orange juice
powdered sugar

Pick flowers clean, wash gently in cool water, and drain. Sift together flour, sugar, and baking powder. Beat eggs, add milk, and mix with dry ingredients. Heat oil to 375° F. Mix flowers into batter and drop by tablespoons into hot oil. Brown both sides of fritters, remove, and drain. Sprinkle with orange juice, dust with powdered sugar, and eat them hot.

Alfred Kinsey's Elderberry Rob

2–3 cups dried elderberries
1 tablespoon cloves
1 tablespoon nutmeg
1 tablespoon cinnamon
½ pound sugar

Boil enough dried berries in water to get 1 quart of juice. Add spices and simmer ½ hour. Strain, and add sugar. Boil for a few minutes, skim, and seal in jars while hot. Poach wild pears in the sauce, or spoon it over other desserts. (Adapted from *M. F. Berry's Fruit Recipes*, published by Doubleday in 1907.)

Stahl's Elder-Blow Wine

8 cups cleaned elder flowers
10 cups sugar
2½ gallons water, boiled and cooled
1 cake yeast
3 pounds raisins

Put flowers and sugar in a 3-gallon crock and fill with the boiled water almost to the top. Float the cake of yeast on top. Cover with a clean cloth and allow to stand 9 days. Then, into each of 3 freshly washed 1-gallon jars put 1 pound of raisins. Strain liquid into the jars, cap loosely, and store in a cool, dark place for 6 months. Decant and strain the liquid into sterilized bottles and cap tightly.

Mark your calendar. At the end of 1 year, chill the wine, pour into champagne glasses, and enjoy.

The next time you ride to the east of Austin, look quickly and you'll find the tiny Wendish village of Serbin. About 7,000 of the world's 100,000 Wends live in Texas, where their ancestors came in the 1850s to escape Prussian discrimination. Yet the Wendish Texans represent one of the smallest, least-known ethnic groups to settle in the state.

Descendants of the Serbs, one of the earliest Slavic tribes to occupy Central Europe in the Middle Ages, the Texan Wends gather annually at their church in Serbin for special religious services, barbecue, sports, and games. Thrifty and self-reliant, they work very hard to keep their religion, costumes, and traditions, such as painting intricate designs on eggshells at Easter. Noodles (see p. 75) they always make, along with preserved figs and, usually, dill pickles. The recipe below is from Evelyn Kasper.

Grandma Fritsche's Figs

1 tablespoon vinegar
1½ cups sugar
1 cup water
2 quarts figs

Bring vinegar, sugar, and water to a boil and add figs. Cook until figs are soft when mashed against the side of the pot with a spoon. Put into hot, sterilized jars and seal. Process 10 minutes in a kettle of boiling water that covers the tops of jars by at least 1 inch.

If you have a good source of Mustang grapes, you probably want to keep it to yourself. The black skins are tough and unpleasant to eat, but Mustangs make good homemade jelly and tasty wine. Old-timers fermented the juice in oak barrels (and some still do), but its most popular use is the dark ruby jelly Texans like on homemade biscuits. Apparently, the hearty *Vitis candicans* and Texas were meant for each other. The grapevine endures heat and drought, its 30- or 40-foot length draped over a tree to create a canopy effect over the clustered grapes.

Here is writer Byron Augustin's method for creating:

Mustang Magic

5 cups strained grape juice
1¾-ounce box fruit pectin (Sure-Jell)
7 cups sugar

To prepare juice: Wash grapes thoroughly; the stems need not be removed. Place washed grapes in a cooker and add enough water to cover them. After the water starts to boil, cook the grapes (stirring frequently) until the skins begin to pop. When the skins will slip easily from the grapes, they are ready to press.

Strain the cooked grapes and juice through a colander lined with a jelly bag or medium textured cloth. Press all of the juice from the grapes with a wooden mallet, but do not force the pulp through the colander.

Add pectin and bring to a rolling boil; add sugar. Stir constantly. Bring the mixture back to a rolling boil and cook for 3–5 minutes. When the mixture forms a string as it is poured from a spoon, remove from heat.

Skim the foam and crystals from the surface, and pour the processed jelly into hot sterilized jars. Seal immediately with canning lids or paraffin before the jelly cools.

Betsy Simpson and her sisters, Carolyn Scrafford and Josephine Sims, can tell you how to jell almost anything that grows in South Texas. Here's a favorite of theirs:

Mustang Grape Jelly

4 cups crushed grapes
¼ cup water
¾–1 cup sugar for each cup juice

Add water to grapes in a big pan. Heat to a boil and simmer 10–15 minutes. Strain through a jelly bag. To prevent crystals in jelly, let the juice stand overnight in a cool place. Dip the crystals out and strain again.

If underripe grapes are used, the juice will be sour; use 1 whole cup sugar to each cup juice. If most of the grapes are ripe, use the ¾ cup measure. Heat juice, add sugar, and stir until sugar is dissolved. Cook until the syrup sheets off a spoon. Pour into hot, sterilized jars and seal at once.

So you didn't know that peanuts are fruit! Few of us gave it a thought until Fayanne Teague reminded us that the peanut is a legume with fruit maturing underground on elongated stalks that push their tips into the soil after the blossoms wither.

But did you know Spanish peanuts were adopted? The Indians introduced the Spaniards to the native American fruit. The Spaniards took them to Africa, where they bought spices and ivory for (you guessed it) *peanuts*. Of course, the plant thrived in Africa, where it was called *nguba*, becoming a nutritional staple in the tribal diet. Then the nguba, or goober, came back to America as cheap food on slave ships. Much later, Dr. George Washington Carver discovered more than 300 uses for the delicious, inexpensive groundnut.

Of those 300 uses, probably everybody's favorite is this, from the Texas Department of Agriculture and Fran Gerling:

Homemade Peanut Butter

1 cup freshly roasted peanuts
3 or more tablespoons peanut oil
½ teaspoon salt

Place the peanuts and 1½ tablespoons peanut oil in an electric blender. Blend until smooth. For salted peanut butter, add ½ teaspoon salt. Gradually add another 1½ tablespoons peanut oil, or enough to make desired consistency. Store in a tightly covered container.

Note: Homemade peanut butter will separate in standing. Stir before using. If you like crunch, add chopped roasted peanuts.

Roasted Peanuts

Spread raw, shelled peanuts in one layer in a shallow baking pan. Heat in a slow oven at 300° F. for 30–45 minutes, depending on how brown you want them. Stir peanuts often as they heat. Check on brownness from time to time by removing the skins from a few of the peanuts. Serve warm.

"Bring your sugar to Oatmeal," they say. Don't bother to look for Oatmeal on the map, but you can find the tiny Central Texas community (population about 20) on F.M. 243, southwest of Bertram.

If you believe that fun depends on city lights, you probably missed the Oatmeal Festival in 1980, the year *Texas Highways* was there. That means you also missed the oatmeal shower, the celebrity dunking, the oatmeal sculpture contest, the Miss Oatmeal Cookie award, the oatmeal cook-off, and more.

Here is a winner:

Peanut Butter Granola

1 cup rolled oats
1 cup coconut
1 cup peanuts
1 cup wheat germ
1 cup sunflower seeds (or sesame seeds)
1 cup whole wheat flour
½ cup water
½ cup oil
½ cup peanut butter
½ cup honey
1 tablespoon vanilla

Combine first six ingredients in a large mixing bowl. Combine remaining ingredients in a saucepan and heat over low heat until melted. Pour over oats mixture. Spread in a 15-by-10-by-1-inch jelly-roll pan. Bake in 350° F. oven for 35–45 minutes, until light brown, stirring every 5–7 minutes.

From *Texas Highways*, November 1979:

Parched Peanuts

For the old-fashioned way: fill a syrup can to within 2 inches of the top rim with raw, unshelled peanuts. Place in a woodburning fireplace, but not in the fire. Heating the can will parch the nuts, but do not place it too close to the fire, or they will burn. Rotate the can every hour, for 4–6 hours, depending on the size of the fireplace and the fire.

Persimmon Marmalade

2 quarts ripe persimmons
1 cup sugar
1 cup orange juice
grated rind of 1 orange

Cut up persimmons; discard seeds and cores. Mash fruit and cook it with sugar, orange juice, and rind until mixture is thick. Seal in hot, sterilized jars. Process 10 minutes in a kettle of boiling water that covers tops of jars by at least 1 inch. Makes about 6 half-pints.

Citrus Relish

2 Ruby Red grapefruit
2 oranges
2 cups sugar
¼ teaspoon cinnamon
¼ teaspoon allspice
1 cup chopped pecans

Wash fruit. Cut into quarters and remove seeds. Do not peel. Put through medium blade of food grinder. Add remaining ingredients and blend. Chill several hours before using. Store in tightly covered container in the refrigerator. Will keep several weeks. Yield: 2 pints.

Frosted Fruit

Use cherries, plums, grapes, apricots, or any small fruit, with stems if possible. Beat 3 egg whites and place in a shallow bowl. Place some fine sugar on a plate. Dip the fruit in the egg white, and then in the sugar. Set in a warm, dry place to harden.

New ways to get your Vitamin C, from the January 1983 *Texas Highways:*

Orange Sherry Cooler

3 cups orange juice
¼ cup sugar
1 cup dry sherry
ice cubes

Mix juice, sugar, and sherry. Serve over ice. Makes eight 4-ounce servings.

During the seventies, a Houston restaurant called the Hobbit Hole began to celebrate Middle Earth, according to the fantasy world of Tolkien. The sandwiches featured egg salad, guacamole, melted cheese, and assorted vegetarian additions. Desserts combined fresh fruits, yogurt and honey dressing, and natural toppings, such as raisins, nuts, and coconut. You

Orange Yogurt Whip, left, and Orange-Banana Wake-up provide two ways to drink a healthful breakfast.

Al Rubio/TDA

can make the favorite drink, the Smoothie, in a blender with whatever fruit you have:

The Smoothie

1½ cups fresh fruit*
1 tablespoon honey
1 tablespoon papaya syrup (optional, for extra sweetness)
2 cups crushed ice

Blend fruit, honey, and papaya syrup in electric blender until smooth. Add ice, and blend just until thick. Makes 1 large or 2 small servings.

*Bananas, strawberries, any fruit in season, or a mixture of favorites.

Orange-Banana Wake-Up

1 egg
1 cup skim milk
3 tablespoons orange juice concentrate
½ banana

Mix ingredients in blender until frothy. Serve immediately in chilled glass. Makes 1 serving.

The seasoning mixtures adapted by Daphne Derven from cookbooks of the 1850s corroborate the old theory that everything under the sun has been there a long time:

Kitchen Pepper

To 4 ounces of cracked black pepper, add 1 ounce of each of the following ground spices: nutmeg, allspice, ginger, and mace, and ½ ounce of ground cloves. Mix thoroughly. Use on meat, fish, and potatoes.

Curry Powder

One ounce each of the following ground spices: turmeric, coriander, cumin, ginger, nutmeg, mace, and cayenne. Mix thoroughly. One teaspoon is the usual amount used.

Herb Powder

Two ounces each of parsley, winter savory, sweet marjoram, and thyme (lemon thyme may be substituted for French thyme); 1 ounce each of sweet basil and finely chopped dried lemon peel. Celery seed and bay leaves are optional (use ¼ ounce each). Mix thoroughly. Rub between the palms of your hands before using.

If you think collecting old recipes is fun, add these to your list. The first came from the Maxey House in Paris, Texas, from the same family that gave us Rock Cookies. Read it for entertainment; it's impossible to make.

Great-Grandmother's Sponge Cake

"Take an odd number of eggs: five or seven make a good-size cake. Of sugar, the weight of the eggs less one egg. Pound the lump of sugar quite fine. Of flour, use half the weight of the sugar. Of some flavor, one tablespoon. If a ship is in, perhaps the juice of a lemon; otherwise, use a light wine.

"Beat separately the whites and yolks, using a silver, not a pewter, fork. Cream together flavor, sugar and half a small pat of fresh, good butter. Put flour in slowly, and fold with eggs. Bake for about half an hour on a fire of not more than two small sticks."

In 1984, when I reviewed an 1850s Christmas in Texas for *Texas Highways*, we paused for a silent moment of thanks for contemporary washing machines, detergents, and bleaches. In 1850, linens were treated to the "celebrated chemical mixture for washing" offered by Elizabeth Waters in *The Ladies Indispensable Assistant*:

The Mixture

½ pound soda
1 gallon boiling water
¼ pound lime
10 ounces common bar soap

Strain and mix the night before. Add to 10 gallons boiling water. Boil three batches of laundry in one mixture, ½ hour each.

Index